The Juilliard Graduate School moves to a new building on Claremont Avenue, adjacent to the IMA building.

The Extension Division (now Evening Division) opens, January 30.

The Master of Science in Music degree program is instituted.

The Juilliard String Quartet is established under the leadership of violinist Robert Mann. Its first members are Mann and Robert Koff, violins; Raphael Hillyer, viola; and Arthur Winograd, cello.

The Institute of Musical Art and the Juilliard Graduate School completely merge to form a single institution.

Martha Hill (at desk) with Myron Nadel and June Dunbar, 1962

Juilliard's Dance Division is established under the direction of Martha Hill (1951–85).

Aaron Copland's *Piano Fantasy*, also commissioned for the school's fiftieth anniversary, is premiered by William Masselos, October 25.

Juilliard accepts an invitation to join Lincoln Center for the Performing Arts as its educational constituent.

1931 1932 1933 1937 1938 1945 1946 1947 1951 1956 1957

The Juilliard Summer School holds its first session. The program, directed by George A. Wedge, is in existence until 1952.

Ernest Hutcheson is appointed president of the Juilliard School of Music (1937–45).

Composer William Howard Schuman, winner of the first Pulitzer Prize for Music, is appointed president of the Juilliard School of Music (1945–61). Among his many accomplishments as president are the complete merger of IMA and JGS, the establishment of the Literature and Materials of Music program, the Juilliard String Quartet, and the Dance Division.

The innovative Literature and Materials of Music curriculum is inaugurated. Schuman's L&M program advocates teaching the elements of music through first-hand study of musical compositions, rather than through a standard text. It had a profound impact on music theory curriculums in colleges and universities throughout the United States. *The Juilliard Report on Teaching the Literature and Materials of Music* was published by W. W. Norton in 1953.

Juilliard celebrates its fiftieth anniversary season with a Festival of American Music, February 10–24. Most of the works performed are commissioned by the Juilliard Musical Foundation for the anniversary season. Commissioned composers include Roger Sessions, Peter Mennin, William Bergsma, Vincent Persichetti, Roy Harris, Vittorio Giannini, and Walter Piston.

Students in Summer School, 1932

Rose Gerringer as Galatea in William Lawes's *Britannia Triumphans*, Festival of British Music at Juilliard, December 1953

JUILLIARD

BY MARO CHERMAYEFF AND AMY SCHEWEL

PREFACE BY JOSEPH W. POLISI

FOREWORD BY FRANK RICH

HARRY N. ABRAMS, INC., PUBLISHERS,

IN ASSOCIATION WITH THIRTEEN/WNET NEW YORK

This volume accompanies *Juilliard*, an *American Masters* program
produced by Thirteen/WNET New York for the Public Broadcasting
Service, executive producer, Susan Lacy

Editor: Harriet Whelchel
Designer: Helene Silverman
Production Manager: Alyn Evans
Consultant for The Juilliard School: Jane Gottlieb

Library of Congress Cataloging-in-Publication Data

Chermayeff, Maro.
 Juilliard / Maro Chermayeff; Amy Schewel.
     p. cm.
"Companion volume to Juilliard, an American Masters program,
executive producer Susan Lacy, produced by Thirteen/WNET/New York
for the Public Broadcasting Service."
Includes index.
 ISBN 0–8109–3536–8
 1. Juilliard School. 2. Conservatories of music—New York
(State)—New York. I. Schewel, Amy. II. Title.
 MT4.N5 J7 2002
 780'.71'17471—dc21

                                    2002002656

Printed and bound in Italy
10 9 8 7 6 5 4 3 2 1

Harry N. Abrams, Inc.
100 Fifth Avenue
New York, N.Y. 10011
www.abramsbooks.com

Abrams is a subsidiary of

Pages 2–3: Drama Group 30, 2001
Page 4: José Límon in studio 610 at Juilliard's Claremont Avenue building, c. 1964

CONTENTS

PREFACE JOSEPH W. POLISI

FOR CLOSE TO twenty years as the president of The Juilliard School, I have continued to be amazed and energized by the excellence that permeates the School's environment: an excellence based on discipline, hard work, the joy of the arts, and profound honesty.

In twenty-first-century America, it is often suggested that expediency is the best way to achieve life goals, but the Juilliard experience exists as a remarkable standard in contrast to such easy solutions. Each year, young dancers, actors, and musicians from around the world come to New York City to audition for the limited places available for the next Juilliard class. Regrettably, the School cannot admit all qualified applicants. Yet, I often hope during these demanding admission days in early March that all who participate in this selective process—applicants, parents, faculty and administrative staff—understand that this experience represents a continuum in the performing arts that has existed for several centuries.

Through this admission process and the education that follows, students are welcomed to a tradition that is at the heart of the performing-arts cycle, involving young people in the development of technique that will support artistic expression. The Juilliard faculty exists to move that tradition forward, taking the very best of the past in dance, drama, and music and applying it to the present, so that tradition and practice will eventually be transformed and re-energized by the next generation of young artists.

Such a venture is a particularly profound, yet subtle process. Balances between innovation and tradition are constantly tested. Acquisition of technique is only one step toward the communicative artistry one looks for in the performing arts. Personal discipline in the arts must not overwhelm the continuous growth of each artist as a young adult. At Juilliard, we look toward the education of not only a complete performing artist, but also a complete human being.

In addition, Juilliard has made a commitment to take an active role in shaping the future of the performing arts, by intensifying its internal commitment to artistic education and by reaching beyond its doors to help the performing arts thrive anew throughout the world. A fundamental goal of the School is to help our students comprehend how art transcends and transforms the human experience, so that the artist can truly function as one of the principal communicators for our world and its values.

These lofty aspirations and traditions vividly come to life in this book. Through never-before published images and an engaging narrative, the reader can experience the personalities and the joy and challenges of the Juilliard experience. As an international institution based in America, we continue to work diligently to provide an educational environment that will prepare the next generation of dancers, actors, and musicians to be leaders in their professions in the time ahead.

Joseph W. Polisi performing with Juilliard faculty and students in Dvorák's Serenade in D Minor, Op. 44, as part of a special concert tribute to Joseph Fuchs, January 18, 1995, Juilliard Theater. Left to right: Ronald Roseman, Monica Johnson, oboes; Joseph W. Polisi, Chad Alexander, bassoons; Douglas Quint, contrabassoon; Iffet Araniti, Julia Pilant, Julie Landsman, horns; Lorne Munroe, cello; Eugene Levinson, double bass; Benjamin Fingland, Alan Kay, clarinets

FOREWORD FRANK RICH

AMERICAN CULTURE, like the nation that is ever reinventing it, is so sprawling and varied that it's hard to imagine how any single institution could encompass it. But such is the nearly century-long history of Juilliard. Born when a young country was first discovering that it might have a serious appetite for the arts, Juilliard grew up with both the country and its burgeoning cultural capital of New York to become an internationally recognized synonym for the pinnacle of artistic achievement.

From its advent as the Institute of Musical Art in 1905, Juilliard knew what it was about. Frank Damrosch, its creator, championed "high standards" in his opening address. As the head of music education for New York's public school system in an era when immigrants were remaking the city, he had the wisdom to seek students of every possible origin, regardless of gender or social class. This was far from a standard vision for the time. High culture in America still meant mainly imported European culture, not the heterogeneous, home-grown brew it would become. Damrosch wanted to inculcate the classical tradition in his students, but in a fertile democratic environment, open to all with the talent and the will to pursue it. This wholly American idea caught on immediately. Planned for 150 students, Damrosch's school had an enrollment of 500 within a year.

What would follow would be a peripatetic history as the Institute of Musical Art moved from the Lenox Mansion on lower Fifth Avenue all the way uptown to Claremont Avenue in Morningside Heights before merging with the Juilliard Graduate School in 1926. In keeping with the expanding cultural map of the city, Juilliard would move to Lincoln Center in 1969. But more revealing than the school's geographical journey is the steady expansion of its artistic portfolio. Dance was added in 1951, then drama in 1968, then jazz. All the while the international reach of the student body was expanding as well. This was surely a formula for explosive creative fusion, and the proof is in the extraordinary range of brilliant alumni, many of whose voices you will hear in the pages that follow.

Whether as students or teachers, the Juilliard roster is in itself a cavalcade of our crazy-quilt artistic history: Richard Rodgers and Kevin Spacey, Leontyne Price and Milton Babbitt, Paul Taylor and Dorothy DeLay, John Houseman and Martha Clarke, Sarah Chang and Robin Williams, William Schuman and Marvin Hamlisch. It's not just that this institution has nurtured so many of the giants in all the arts, but in true American fashion, it has nurtured high and pop culture alike, from the Met and the Philharmonic to Broadway and Hollywood. It has also, again in the best American tradition, forged pioneers and leaders who have fanned out throughout the country and the world to bring Damrosch's "high standards" to every conceivable performing-arts arena. Under its modern leader, Joseph W. Polisi, the ideals of artistic citizenship and advocacy have been added to Juilliard's repertoire, and you see those ideals being carried forward everywhere by the school's progeny, from the national educational mission of Wynton Marsalis to the remaking of Shakespearean theater under Michael Kahn's auspices in Washington. Juilliard is, as you will see, an epic story, but a quintessentially American epic of perennial reinvention, with thrilling new chapters being added every day.

David Ogden Stiers, left, and Jed Sakren, right, in Molière's *Scapin* directed by Pierre Lefevre, 1972. At far left is Patti LuPone. Also pictured are Gerald Gutierrez (behind Stiers) and David Schramm (far right).

I THINK that when Frank Damrosch founded the Institute of Musical Art in 1905…the idea of an *American* music was still something that was very provocative because American classical music was really borrowed European music at that point. Going back to 1905, one of the things Damrosch wanted to do was to provide a climate in which American music could develop and in which American performers could study without having to leave the country.
BRUCE BRUBAKER

The Lenox mansion on Twelfth Street and Fifth Avenue, New York City, the original home of the Institute of Musical Art, c. 1905

THE INSTITUTE OF
MUSICAL ART

THE SCHOOL became very much an expression of Frank's personality I would say… in that it was extraordinarily proper —you had to wear your hat in school if you were a man…. The faculty wore black tie and tails to the final exams every year…. You would stand up if the director came into the room. But, at the same time the school was extraordinarily free of social pretension. From the beginning, in the charter of the school, it was explicit that it was open to both genders, to people irrespective of race, creed, or color. Social class was of no importance at all. A scholarship fund was established from the very beginning. It was very important to their work. So in that sense it was both a model of very Victorian propriety but also had a very broad-based social vision that it would be the whole of American society that could come into the school. **DAVID DAMROSCH**

Top: *The New York Times*, October 8, 1905. This article appeared a few weeks before the formal opening of the Institute, on Tuesday, October 31, 1905 at four o'clock. The opening ceremony at the Lenox mansion featured a program of music and speeches, including an address by Woodrow Wilson, president of Princeton University and later president of the United States.

Above: *The New York Times*, March 24, 1905

Opposite: An excerpt from Frank Damrosch's address at the June 5, 1906, commencement, which marked the formal conclusion of the Institute's first year.

Address, Frank Damrosch
June 5, 1906

Students, Ladies, and Gentlemen:

What we need is a school here where the needs of every student shall be recognized and fulfilled.... We are going to continue our work next year with the object of giving to all talented students an opportunity to develop their talents to the fullest extent. But there are students who are not great and pronounced talents. We love them too and we will provide for them, too. They are here because they love music so dearly that they want to know all about it. We shall take good care of them. Sometimes the people who think they are destined to become virtuosos and to show the world what wonderful things they can do are under the conviction that a school which exists only for them is the only right place for them.... What I want to accomplish with this school is to set high standards of musical appreciation, or musical performance, or art in music, which shall not only be demonstrated by the performance of the individual, but also by the appreciation of the art work itself. That is more important to us than anything else, for as it has been said a great poet can only be appreciated by poets, so it is with the great in the art of music. Not alone the great artist, the great art work can only be appreciated by those who have become *musicians*. And it is so easy to become a *musician*.... You smile when you think of the hours and hours of practice you devoted to it, but that is not what made you musicians. That is what made you piano players and fiddlers, but not musicians. What made you musicians is the love and understanding of music. Meet music halfway. What I want to do is to make people put music into their lives as a necessity, not as a luxury; as something without which they cannot exist—for we cannot live without the beautiful and remain human. I want all people who love music to study it thoroughly, and then I want those who have been gifted by the Creator with special musical gifts to come into this atmosphere of people who are all in love with this art, and under the influences of such an atmosphere, to become *musicians*. And then they will be more than piano players, fiddlers, and shouters. They will be really *musicians*. They will become interpreters of the great works of musical art instead of exploiters of their little selves.

FRANK DAMROSCH

The Baton

Published by and for the Students of the Institute of Musical Art of the City of New York
FRANK DAMROSCH, *Director*

Vol. II—No. 1   OCTOBER, 1922   *15 Cents a Copy*

AMONG THE HIGH ALPS

By Frank Damrosch

The Editor of The Baton is a hard task-master and her commands must be obeyed though the storm-tossed ship rolls and pitches in the great, angry waves piled up by the hurricane. How I wished that I had written this account of my travels while *terra firma* still gave steady support to my pen and while my brain was capable of concentrated thought instead of reeling with the wild motion of the ever heaving and again sudden dipping of the deck. Moreover, I am expected to tell the readers of The Baton about my musical experiences in Europe and—let me whisper a secret in your ears—I haven't had any, because (oh shame and horror) I have run away from them! Only once,—but that is another story.

My object in going to Europe this summer was threefold: firstly, to meet again many old friends whom I had not seen since 1914; secondly, to study present conditions in Europe and finally, to rest my nerves after listening during the past eight years to 8465 candidates for admission to the Institute, holding 11,473 classroom examinations, conducting 764 orchestra and chorus rehearsals, seeing a million people about a million things and hearing the students in room H trying to play the piano every day and all day while Mr. Kneisel is stamping rhythm into his pupils on my devoted head. You

The Corvatch Peak near St. Moritz, Switzerland

On Top

(Continued on page 2)

FOLK MUSIC AND ITS TEACHINGS

By H. E. Krehbiel

How can a student of the Institute of Musical Art profit from the study of folksongs? I have found that they have shown unusual interest in the series of talks on the subject which are a feature of my lectures on musical appreciation, but have sometimes thought that this was because of the charm of the illustrations. Of course a teacher is always gratified at any evidence that he has found a means of holding the attention of his class, but there is a drop of bitterness in his satisfaction if he discovers, or even suspects, that what he designed to be instruction is received as passing entertainment merely.

In music it is only hearing that is believing. Training brings with it the capacity to hear with the mental ear, it is true, and this capacity should be sedulously cultivated; but the best of composers is most truly contented when after hearing a performance of an orchestral piece of his writing, he can say to himself, "It sounds well!" He has then, if he has written well, had his imaginings and intentions confirmed by the only sense to which music can appeal. When the poet talks about unheard melodies being sweeter than those which enter the physical ear, he is talking fantastic hyperbole; and there is a monstrous deal of such writing in poems, romances and essays. Words can call up images in the mind of things that have been seen by the eye or

(Continued on page 3)

I AM expected to tell the readers of *The Baton* about my musical experiences in Europe this summer…. My object in going to Europe was threefold: firstly, to meet again many old friends whom I had not seen since 1914; secondly, to study present conditions in Europe, and, finally, to rest my nerves after listening during the past eight years to 8,465 candidates for admission to the Institute, holding 11,473 classroom examinations, conducting 764 orchestra and chorus rehearsals, seeing a million people about a million things and hearing the students in room H trying to play the piano every day and all day while Mr. Kneisel is stamping rhythm into his pupils on my devoted head. **FRANK DAMROSCH**

IF YOU look back at these early publications like *The Baton* or *Harmonics*, they included stories about what would seem to us to be the personal lives of the faculty…but I think that kind of encapsulates the attitude or the atmosphere that was part of the school, then…that it was this kind of *club*—and that the students were admitted and that they could be part of this, too, and that it was a wonderful kind of comradeship. I don't know that that atmosphere prevails anymore. **BRUCE BRUBAKER**

Above: James Loeb at his desk. The son of a prominent banking family, Loeb entered the family firm of Kuhn, Loeb & Company after his graduation from Harvard in 1888. In 1901, he retired from business to devote himself to cultural and scholarly interests. He founded the Loeb Classical Library, a series of English translations of classical Greek and Latin texts published by Harvard University Press. An amateur cellist, Loeb provided the original $500,000 endowment for the Institute of Musical Art.

Opposite: *The Baton* was a publication of the Institute of Musical Art from January 1922 through June of 1932. This well-illustrated periodical appeared approximately eight to nine times during the academic year, and contained articles of musical interest and news of the Institute. Produced by both students and faculty, it offered a spirited and eclectic mix of essays and letters.

CLAREMONT AVENUE

IN 1910, THE INSTITUTE OF MUSICAL ART (IMA) MOVED TO A NEW HOME ON CLAREMONT AVENUE AND 122ND STREET AND REMAINED AT THIS SITE UNTIL ITS MOVE TO LINCOLN CENTER IN 1969. IN THE NEARLY SIXTY YEARS AT THIS LOCATION, THE SCHOOL AND THE BUILDING EXPANDED AND DEVELOPED TO ACCOMMODATE A MAJOR MERGER THAT PROPELLED THE INSTITUTION FORWARD GIVING IT AN EVEN GRANDER PROFILE IN THE WORLD OF PERFORMING ARTS.

THEY DIDN'T stay very long at the first building on Fifth Avenue because they outgrew it. Frank Damrosch had a really radically new idea pedagogically and for a whole community, so he needed to build a building that would embody it. Not only to have enough practice rooms but also to have common spaces, a cafeteria so people could have their lunch there and never leave, and to have a concert hall so that the students could have concerts presented there by visiting artists as well as their own concerts. He had everything together under one roof for an entire musical experience.
DAVID DAMROSCH

1905 — 1930

THE SCHOOL building was very old with paneled walls, and you felt like you were going back into history, as if you were going to meet Beethoven.
WILLIAM VACCHIANO

IN THE old building at 122nd Street there were practice rooms and they had double doors so that everybody could play and practice without disturbing the other people down the hall. So I'd be inside, supposedly practicing but really playing the score from *Gypsy* or *My Fair Lady*. And if I heard the first door open up, I would immediately go into Bach, knowing that by the second door the teacher would walk in and say, "How's it going?" You know? So, it was a very clandestine thing that I was doing, which was to love Broadway. **MARVIN HAMLISCH**

WHAT A lovely little building.... I remember looking out the window, and it looked a little bit like Paris up in that area. There were big trees. I remember with fondness the light from one angle of the big dance studio looking down over those treetops. I can't bear to work in rooms without windows, so I'm glad I was in that generation and the old building. **MARTHA CLARKE**

Opposite, above: Program cover for the celebration of the twenty-fifth anniversary of the Institute of Musical Art, at the Commodore Hotel, April 2, 1930

Opposite, below: The main hall of the Institute of Musical Art on Claremont Avenue; adjoining is the office of director, Frank Damrosch

Overleaf: The twenty-fifth anniversary dinner celebration on April 2, 1930, included between four hundred and five hundred guests. Seated at the speaker's table were members of the faculty, administration, and board of trustees, including (left to right) Rubin Goldmark, Percy Goetschius, Ernest Hutcheson, Rosina Lhévinne, Arthur Cox, Mrs. Franz Kneisel, Frank Damrosch, Mrs. Arthur Cox, John Erskine, Mrs. Frank Damrosch, John L. Wilkie, Mrs. Ernest Hutcheson, Gardner Lawson, Anna Duncan, Mischa Levitzki, Josef Lhévinne, George A. Wedge, and Carl Engel. Among the other distinguished guests were David Mannes (founder of Mannes College of Music) and philanthropists Harry Harkness Flagler and Otto H. Kahn.

APRIL - - - 1940

HARMONICS

INSTITUTE OF MUSICAL ART
OF THE
JUILLIARD SCHOOL of MUSIC

IT FELT like a wonderful old black-and-white movie … there was such character to it … you know … gaslit, and the woman in the coatroom where you'd hand her your coats had a matron's outfit on. There was an elevator person with white gloves. It was really quite fabulous, from another time…. So you walked in there thinking, "Wow! Where am I going? This is great!" **MARK SNOW**

13

DINNER TO CELEBRATE THE
TWENTY-FIFTH ANNIVERSARY
OF THE
FOUNDING OF THE INSTITUTE OF MUSICAL ART
HOTEL COMMODORE — APRIL 2, 1930

30

THE JUILLIARD GRADUATE SCHOOL

AT THE SAME TIME THAT THE INSTITUTE OF MUSICAL ART FLOURISHED AND CARRIED OUT ITS MISSION ON CLAREMONT AVENUE, DOWN ON EAST 52ND STREET, A NEW MUSICAL INSTITUTION WAS JUST BEGINNING. THE JUILLIARD GRADUATE SCHOOL WAS CREATED BY THE JUILLIARD MUSICAL FOUNDATION, ENDOWED BY AUGUSTUS D. JUILLIARD, WHO WISHED TO ADVANCE MUSICAL EDUCATION IN THE UNITED STATES. THESE TWO INSTITUTIONS WOULD LATER MERGE TO CREATE THE SCHOOL THE WORLD KNOWS TODAY SIMPLY AS JUILLIARD.

THE JUILLIARD Graduate School was small. They had enough string players to have one symphony orchestra, they had an opera department, and that was it. There was, at that time, no drama, no dance division. It was an all-scholarship school and the student body was primarily American. The faculty was primarily European and the teachers were from Russia, Germany, England, many different countries. Of course, that has changed tremendously because now we have a predominance of Asian and European students and the teachers are mostly American. It has really turned around!
DOROTHY DELAY

Members of the Juilliard Graduate School faculty, November 1928. Seated, left to right: Rosina Lhévinne, Olga Samaroff, Leopold Auer, Ernest Hutcheson, Marcella Sembrich, Paul Kochanski, Anna E. Schoen-René, and Rubin Goldmark. Standing left to right: Franklin Robinson, Felix Salmond, Oscar Wagner, Paul Reimers, James Friskin, Carl Friedburg, Francis Rodgers, and Edouard Dethier, Alexander Siloti, Minna Saumelle, Rhoda Erskine, Florence Kimball, Hans Letz, and Bernard Wagenaar. Not present when this photograph was taken were faculty members Albert Stoessel, Alfredo Valenti, Josef Lhévinne, and Georges Barrère. Louis Persinger later joined the violin faculty, replacing Leopold Auer.

Below: Textile magnate Augustus D. Juilliard was born in 1836 to a French family who emigrated to the United States in that same year. Over his lifetime, he made contributions to enrich both the commercial and artistic life in America. Upon his death in 1919, he made a surprising bequest—estimated at $15 million, the largest single gift of this kind to date—toward the establishment of the Juilliard Musical Foundation, for the advancement of musical education.

$10,000,000 TO GO TO AMERICAN MUSIC

Juilliard Foundation Receives Fund Provided by Will to Educate Youth.

TO OUTLINE PLANS LATER

Trustees Have Consulted Hundreds of Persons and Organizations as to Methods.

More than $10,000,000 has been received by the Juilliard Musical Foundation formed by the will of the lat

JUILLIARD STARTED in the Vanderbilt Guest House, an elegant structure of five or six floors with a beautiful stairwell of Carrara marble and a European-style lift, operated by a small, old man named Carey. The second floor was spacious and flanked on either side by an enormous room with beautiful Oriental carpets, French door windows, Steinways, and a bathroom with bathtubs. The sixth floor was the servant's quarters, small rooms that were used as practice rooms with male students on the right and female students on the left. With the coed meshing and merging in the last twenty-five years, this seems like something out of a Jane Austen novel. We did not work for degrees and everyone there (around 135 students) felt special, and that he or she was going to be a great performer; let the students at the Institute of Musical Art and Peabody or Eastman get the degrees. Who needed a degree? We were going to be performers. **JOSEF RAIEFF**

Above: The front door of the Juilliard Graduate School

Left: *The New York Times*, February 23, 1923

Opposite: In 1924, the trustees of the Juilliard Foundation created a school for advanced musical students. The Vanderbilt Guest House, 49 East 52nd Street in New York City, was the first home of the Juilliard Graduate School.

THERE WAS no government support for the arts. There was very little interest in musical culture. Most of these [musical education] ventures involved finding some patron who could really get them started. Frank Damrosch repeatedly tried to get Andrew Carnegie and all sorts of other people to increase the endowment of the school [the IMA] with no success, and the $500,000 dollars that Loeb provided kept him going at a modest level. But the school could never grow the way he had hoped because there simply weren't funds, and he wanted to keep tuition quite low so that a broad base of people could go to it. This certainly influenced the merger with Juilliard, when that came about, since what we had was a thriving school with no endowment, which met a thriving endowment with no school. **DAVID DAMROSCH**

Right: John Erskine (left) and Ernest Hutcheson (right). Columbia University professor John Erskine was an amateur pianist and prolific author who published more than twenty-five books on a variety of subjects; his 1950 memoir, *My Life in Music*, includes his firsthand perspectives on the early years of the Juilliard School of Music. A pianist and composer, Australian-born Hutcheson had been head of the piano department at the Peabody Conservatory in Baltimore before coming to Juilliard. In 1937, he succeeded Erskine as President of the Juilliard School of Music, and remained in this position until 1945.

Far right: In 1931 the Juilliard Graduate School moved to a new building at 130 Claremont Avenue, adjacent to the IMA building. The new building was designed by Shreve, Lamb, and Harmon, the same architectural firm that designed the Empire State building. To mark the occasion, Leopold Stokowski conducted the combined IMA and JGS orchestras on November 7, and Sergei Rachmaninoff presented a solo piano recital on November 12.

MERGER OF THE JUILLIARD GRADUATE SCHOOL AND THE INSTITUTE OF MUSICAL ART

IN 1926, THE JUILLIARD SCHOOL OF MUSIC WAS CREATED THROUGH A MERGER OF THE INSTITUTE OF MUSICAL ART AND THE JUILLIARD GRADUATE SCHOOL. THE GRADUATE SCHOOL WAS REORGANIZED, AND, IN 1927, ERNEST HUTCHESON WAS NAMED ITS DEAN. IN 1928, JOHN ERSKINE BECAME THE FIRST PRESIDENT OF THE COMBINED INSTITUTIONS. WHEN DAMROSCH RESIGNED AS DEAN OF IMA IN 1933 DUE TO ILLNESS, HUTCHESON WAS APPOINTED DEAN OF BOTH IMA AND JGS. ALTHOUGH THE TWO SCHOOLS WERE BY THEN UNITED UNDER ONE ROOF, THEY MAINTAINED SEPARATE ENTRANCES, FACULTIES, AND STUDENT BODIES. THE INSTITUTE OF MUSICAL ART GRANTED FORMAL DEGREES AND CHARGED TUITION; THE JUILLIARD GRADUATE SCHOOL WAS THE MORE "ELITIST" OF THE TWO SCHOOLS, OFFERING FULLY FUNDED FELLOWSHIPS TO TALENTED MUSICIANS AND ALLOWING THEM TO STUDY WITH PROMINENT ARTIST-TEACHERS WITHOUT OTHER CURRICULAR REQUIREMENTS. THE FULL AMALGAMATION OF THE TWO INSTITUTIONS WAS NOT COMPLETED UNTIL 1946, UNDER THE PRESIDENCY OF WILLIAM SCHUMAN.

IN THIS ISSUE: WHAT ENGLAND HEARS—By Eugene Goossens
SOME SKRYABIN LETTERS TO ALTSCHULER

MUSICAL COURIER
Weekly Review OF THE World's Music

Subscription $5.00 Europe $6.25 Annually   NEW YORK, SATURDAY, OCTOBER 10, 1931   Price 15 Cents

A Corner in the Office of Ernest Hutcheson.

Photo by Harold Wagner
JOHN ERSKINE,
President, Juilliard School of Music.

Office of John Erskine.

ERNEST HUTCHESON,
Dean, Juilliard Graduate School.

The Students' Lounge.

DR. FRANK DAMROSCH,
Dean, Institute of Musical Art.

Office of Oscar Wagner.

Photo by Albert Peterson
OSCAR WAGNER,
Assistant Dean, Juilliard School of Music.

Office of Olga Samaroff, Director of Extension Department.

Interior Views of the Newly-Completed Juilliard School of Music

Interiors by Elsie Sloan Farley   Photos of Interiors by Samuel H. Gottscho

It's a very busy SEASON at the JUILLIARD SCHOOL

This is the entrance to the Juilliard Graduate School through which one enters to the . . .

THE Juilliard Graduate School of Music, New York, announces its ever-growing activities by merely noting an unprecedented list of excellent engagements for the last few weeks of 1928 and the first two weeks of January, 1929.

Seventy-four events by seventy-nine students and faculty members are recorded. These include solo recitals, joint-recitals, orchestral appearances as vocalists and instrumentalists, and also as composers.

Professor John Erskine, president of the Juilliard School, appeared on Dec. 2 as assisting artist with the Musical Art Quartet. Ernest Hutcheson, dean of the Graduate School, gave a piano recital in Baltimore on Dec. 7 and was heard in a delightful three-piano concert with Guy Maier and Lee Pattison in Kansas City on Dec. 11. On Dec. 13 and 14 he was soloist with the Minneapolis Symphony Orchestra in Minneapolis.

CARL FRIEDBERG gave four piano recitals in sixteen days. These were on Dec. 4 in Joplin, Mo.; on Dec. 14 and 15 in San Francisco, and on Dec. 20 in Santa Barbara, Cal. On Jan. 11 Mr. Friedberg gave a recital in Carnegie Hall, New York.

Paul Kochanski gave six violin recitals in December; on the third in Corinth, N. Y., on the seventh and eighth in Newcastle, Pa., on the tenth in East Liverpool, Pa., and the next day in Bradford, Pa. On Dec. 13 he gave two recitals in Pittsburgh.

Francis Rogers sang on Dec. 20 in the Library of Congress, Washington. James Friskin, pianist, was soloist on Jan. 13 with the New Haven Symphony Orchestra. Isabelle Addis, singer, appeared on Dec. 23 as soloist at Fort Washington Collegiate Church, and on Dec. 25 sang over the radio at Station WJZ. Ethel Aaron, singer, a former student of the School, gave a recital in Brooklyn, on Dec. 8, accompanied by Gwendolyn Ashbaugh who is a Juilliard student.

Nicolai Berzowsky, who sits at the first desk of the second violins with the Philharmonic Orchestra, had his Hebrew Suite played by the Philharmonic-Symphony on Dec. 7. On Dec. 19 the League of Composers presented his Suite for Wind Instruments. Pearl Besuner sang the role of Siebel in Faust at the Metropolitan Opera on Dec. 8, and appeared in the same part on Dec. 25 in Brooklyn. Kurtis Brownell, singer, was soloist at the Men's Bible Club in White Plains, N. Y., on Dec. 28. Janice Davenport gave a song recital at the Three Arts Club in New York on Dec. 16. Michael de Stefano, violinist, was soloist at the Marble Collegiate Church in New York on Dec. 23, and on Dec. 30 was soloist at St. Mark's Methodist Episcopal Church in Brooklyn.

salon and reception room, used for recitals and school activities, and in which one is quite likely to meet . . .

Philip Duey sang on the General Motors Radio Hour over WEAF as soloist and in the trio on Dec. 10. On Dec. 15 he sang with the trio at the Park Central Hotel in New York; and on Dec. 18 was heard on the Ever-ready Radio Hour over WEAF, both as soloist and with the trio. Sonia Essin gave a recital at the Park Royal Hotel, New York, on Dec. 19, accompanied by Rudolph Gruen, also a Juilliard student. Edwina Eustis sang over WOR with the Rutgers Glee Club on Dec. 12.

Susan Fisher gave a song recital on Dec. 6 at Southold, L. I., and on Dec. 7 was soloist in a Saint-Saens cantata at Rutgers University. On Dec. 16 she was soloist in a Bach Cantata at Princeton University, N. J. Louise Florea, singer, appeared as soloist at McMillan Hall in Columbia University, N. Y., on Dec. 11th, and on Dec. 28 gave a song recital for the Annie Louise Cary Club Scholarship Fund in Gorham, Me. Inga Hill gave a song recital for Mrs. Carpenter in Minneapolis on Dec. 25.

Dorothy Kendrick, pianist, gave a recital on Dec. 9 in the Barbizon Hotel. On Dec. 11 she appeared in recital at the Wanamaker Auditorium. Muriel Kerr appeared on Dec. 5 as piano soloist with the Philharmonic-Symphony Orchestra under Willem Mengelberg at the inaugural concert of Schubert Memorial at arnegie Hall in New York, and on Dec. 9 gave a recital for the Educational Alliance, substituting for Ernest Schelling on a last minute call. Dorys LeVene, pianist, gave a sonata recital in Steinway Hall on Dec. 18. Adel Marcus was heard on Dec. 20 in a piano recital at the Community Center, Far Rockaway, N. Y.

Winifred Michaelson, pianist, appeared at the Friday Morning Music Club in Washington on Dec. 29. Nella Miller, pianist, appeared in a concert for Mrs. Prentice in Cleveland on Dec. 13, and on Dec. 14 was heard at the Cleveland Institute of Music. On Dec. 20 she appeared at Hartford, Conn. Ruth Negaard, singer, gave a recital for the N. Y. U. Children's Christmas party at the School of Commerce on Dec. 20.

Another Juilliard Graduate School orchestral concert was given at the Engineering Auditorium on Dec. 15 with Albert Stoessel as conductor, and with five Juilliard students as soloists; —Hine Brown, violinist; Harry Fagin, violinist; John Frazer, 'cellist; Thomas Mancini, violinist, and Jacques Singer, violinist.

Solomon Pimsleur, a pianist-composer and former Juilliard student, gave a recital of his own compositions at the Engineering Auditorium on Dec. 22. Helen Riley, singer, was heard at Southold, L. I., on Dec. 6, and on Dec. 9 was soloist in a cantata by Saint-Saens at Rutgers University. On Dec. 25 she appeared as soloist with the Cathedral Choir in Syracuse, N. Y., and on Dec. 16 she was soloist in a Bach Cantata at Princeton, N. J.

Marion Sele was the solo singer on Dec. 17 with the Women's University Glee Club in Town Hall, New York, and was soloist in a Bach cantata concert at Princeton, N. J., on Dec. 16. Ruth Shefkowitz appeared as soloist at Adelphi College in Brooklyn, on Dec. 21.

Sadah Shuchari, violinist, gave a recital at the Barbizon Hotel on Dec. 2 and on Dec. 5 was the soloist with the Philharmonic-Symphony Orchestra under Willem Mengelberg at the inaugural concert of the Schubert Memorial, Inc., at Carnegie Hall. Pauline Sternlicht gave a two-piano recital with Etta Kabram, a former student, at the Philadelphia Conservatory of Music on Dec. 17.

A STUDENT recital was given in the Graduate School at 49 East Fifty-second Street, on Dec. 7. Seven students appeared, the first four being from Mr. Letz's ensemble class. They were: Charles Lichter, violinist; Hine Brown, violinist; Solomon Deutsch, viola player, and Katherine Fletcher, 'cellist. The other three were; Susan Fisher, singer; Marcus Gordon, pianist, and Harry Katzman, violinist.

There was a second student recital at the Graduate School on Dec. 21, when the soloists were Bernard Gabriel, pianist; John Kuebler, singer; Mary Huggins, pianist, and Lucrezia Avella, violinist.

Carl Theman, singer, appeared as soloist in the Bach Cantata Concert at Princeton, N. J., on Dec. 16. Erwin Yaeckel, pianist, gave a recital on Dec. 20 for the Fortnightly Club at Hornell, N. Y. Isabelle Yalkovsky, appeared as piano soloist with the Philadelphia Orchestra, in the Metropolitan Opera House, Philadelphia, on Dec. 2. On Jan. 2 Isabelle Yalkowsky appeared as soloist with the Philharmonic-Symphony Orchestra under Ossip Gabrilowitsch at the second Schubert Memorial concert in Carnegie Hall.

Janice Davenport sang the role of Anna in The Merry Wives of Windsor with the Little Theatre Opera Company in Brooklyn, and in New York. The production opened on Jan. 14 for a four week's run. Gladys de Almeida, soprano, gave a recital in Boston on Jan. 5. Evan Evans, baritone, and Carl Theman, were announced to sing in The Merry Wives of Windsor with the Little Theatre Opera Company in Brooklyn and New York for four weeks.

Muriel Kerr, pianist, will make her solo debut on Jan. 31 in a Town Hall recital, New York.

the dean of the school, Ernest Hutcheson.

Musical America January 26, 1929, article about the Juilliard Graduate School

A portrait of the stringed-instrument students as seen in the Juilliard publication *Harmonics*, May 1939. Standing fourth from the left is young Robert Mann, who went on to become a founding member of the famed Juilliard String Quartet.

CERTAINLY originally there was no intent to merge the Juilliard Graduate School and Institute of Musical Art. They saw themselves as two institutions with different missions joined by a common language of music. But financially they were really forced to come together. Of course, this was the Great Depression and they had to find the resources to continue to exist…and the resources were clearly on the Juilliard Graduate School side. **JOSEPH W. POLISI**

WHEN I finished high school, it was ordained…. You know, everybody went to study in either New York or Los Angeles or places like that, and I thought I would enroll in the Juilliard [Graduate] School. It turned out that I had the addresses wrong and I had applied to enter the Institute of Musical Art. But I went, and ended up studying with Mr. Edouard Dethier in the Institute. Prior to that point I had had no, shall we say, proper musical training. **ROBERT MANN**

29

ORCHESTRA

ORCHESTRAL PERFORMANCE HAS ALWAYS BEEN A CENTRAL COMPONENT OF MUSICAL STUDY AT JUILLIARD AND ITS PREDECESSOR INSTITUTIONS, THE INSTITUTE OF MUSICAL ART AND THE JUILLIARD GRADUATE SCHOOL. THROUGHOUT THE YEARS, JUILLIARD MUSICIANS HAVE GONE ON TO HOLD SEATS IN MOST OF THE GREAT ORCHESTRAS OF THE WORLD.

Michael Christie conducting the Juilliard Orchestra with solo violinist Tai Murray in Prokofiev's Violin Concert No. 2 in G Minor, Op. 63, at the May 23, 2002 Commencement Concert in Alice Tully Hall. The program also included Smetana's Overture to *The Bartered Bride* and Lutoslawski's Concerto for Orchestra.

AT JUILLIARD, what I was able to develop was the sharing of music with your friends…that's why I always loved orchestra…. When you put it all together and you hear it happening, it's like eating a fantastic meal when you're starving. I was making music with my friends, and there was nothing greater. **NADJA SALERNO-SONNENBERG**

Opposite: Juilliard Orchestra backstage during a concert intermission, c. 1957

Above: Backstage before a Juilliard Choral Union and Orchestra concert at Alice Tully Hall, April 5, 2002. In the foreground are violinists Dort Bigg (left) and Wayne Lee.

Left: The Juilliard Orchestra on tour in Europe in 1958: students Michael Yurgeles, Noel Gilbert, and Albert Wehr outside Town Hall, Tumbridge Wells, England

KIDS WOULD show up from all over the world and have all kinds of personalities—naïve, sophisticated, quiet, aggressive, happy, friendly, depressed, everything—and it didn't seem to matter, their talent was visited upon them whether they wanted it or not. The oboe players, the flutists, the brass players all seemed to have a personality that was similar. The brass players seemed to be, as a group, blue-collar guys who would go and get drunk and raise hell. The string players were sort of anally nasty and neat. The woodwind players were sort of neurotic and could go either way. So, cliques were sometimes dictated by our instrument. **MARK SNOW**

Above: Orchestra reading with Sir Colin Davis, December 9, 1997

Opposite: Born in Germany in 1926, conductor Otto-Werner Mueller helped shape the orchestral training programs of distinguished musical institutions in the United States and Canada. After studying conducting, composition, piano, trumpet, and viola in Frankfurt, Germany, he emigrated to Canada in 1951 and has worked extensively throughout the world. Mr. Mueller has been on the Juilliard faculty since 1987 and is currently Director of Orchestral Studies.

THE WAY Juilliard affected me, coming out of a liberal arts school where there was really no competition at all, was that suddenly I was thrown into a competitive atmosphere…strata were defined immediately. The first orchestra was the best, the second orchestra wasn't the best…everybody knew where they stacked up on the totem pole. And for me, that was somewhat daunting. I must have a competitive component because I kind of threw myself into it and I realized—and maybe it's the first time it clicked in for me—that you really have to do the work. It's one thing to be a talented kid, going to a liberal arts school and getting to play a recital for your peers, and it's another thing to be at Juilliard where the best of the best have come.
EUGENIA ZUKERMAN

James DePreist conducting the
Juilliard Symphony, Avery Fisher
Hall, March 24, 1999, in the
world-premiere performance of
Michael White's Viola Concerto,
with student soloist Masumi Per
Rostad. Michael White teaches
Literature and Materials of
Music and graduate courses at
Juilliard.

OPERA AND VOCAL

ARTS

The Juilliard School
1985—1986 Season

JUILLIARD AMERICAN OPERA CENTER

★ AN OPERA GALA ★

★ ENSEMBLES FROM GRAND OPERA ★
A Serenade to William Schuman in honor of his 75th birthday

★ CASEY AT THE BAT ★
A Baseball Cantata by William Schuman
NEW YORK PREMIERE

Friday, November 22, 1985 at 8:00 p.m.
Sunday, November 24, 1985 at 3:00 p.m.
THE JUILLIARD THEATER, 155 WEST 65th STREET

I DON'T think it's possible for a conservatory to be a great conservatory without an opera program. And there were always fully produced operas at Juilliard throughout the decades.
JOSEPH W. POLISI

© Beth Bergman

Above: The program cover of an opera gala presented by the Juilliard American Opera Center. This event, in November 1985, celebrated William Schuman's seventy-fifth birthday and featured the New York premiere of his *Casey at the Bat*.

Left: Renée Fleming in *Casey at the Bat*. While Fleming was a student at Juilliard she studied with Beverley Johnson.

Above: *Hansel and Gretel*, December 1997. The Juilliard Opera Center's production of this opera by Engelbert Humperdinck was directed by Frank Corsaro, with sets and costumes by Maurice Sendak. The production was featured as a "Live from Lincoln Center" broadcast on December 17.

Above: *Hansel and Gretel*, 1929. Beatrice Hegt (left) played Hansel and M. Catherine Akins was Gretel.

Left: The 1934 production of Richard Strauss's *Ariadne auf Naxos*, featuring Risë Stevens

© Beth Bergman

THE REASON the human voice is probably the most popular of the musical instruments, is because it is so personal. It has *you* in it. It is *you*, and you go to the audience. And if you enjoy that, it is not only the thrill of a lifetime, but it is a journey that never stops.
LEONTYNE PRICE

Left: Fight scene from Juilliard Opera Center's production of *Hugh the Drover*, by Ralph Vaughan Williams, April 1990

Below: A 1952 production of *Falstaff* at Juilliard featured a young singer, Mary Leontyne Price, in the role of Mistress Ford.

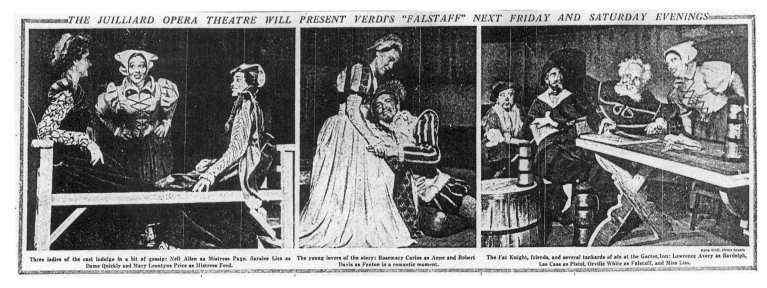

THE JUILLIARD OPERA THEATRE WILL PRESENT VERDI'S "FALSTAFF" NEXT FRIDAY AND SATURDAY EVENINGS

Three ladies of the cast indulge in a bit of gossip: Nell Allen as Mistress Page, Saralee Liss as Dame Quickly and Mary Leontyne Price as Mistress Ford.

The young lovers of the story: Rosemary Carlos as Anne and Robert Davis as Fenton in a romantic moment.

The Fat Knight, friends, and several tankards of ale at the Garter, Inn: Lawrence Avery as Bardolph, Lee Cass as Pistol, Orville White as Falstaff, and Miss Liss.

I ENJOY seeing someone in the first year fighting and trying to amalgamate the vocal techniques with their own private technique…essentially what I'm after is that they own their music. As I've often said to them, why should I pay $75 or, pardon me, $140 to hear you sing? What are you going to say to me that I don't know? That can only come from what *you* know, what *you* can share with us. So it's that ownership that I work at with them.

FRANK CORSARO

Above: Tito Capobianco, director of Juilliard's American Opera Center from 1969 to 1970, with Leonard Bernstein during rehearsal of Beethoven's *Fidelio*. A concert version of this work was performed jointly by the New York Philharmonic and the American Opera Center in January 1970, in honor of Juilliard's first year at Lincoln Center.

Opposite (left to right): Opera faculty member Alfredo Valenti, conductor Edgar Schenkman, and designer Frederick Kiesler during rehearsals for Weber's *Der Freischütz*, December 1946. Renowned architect and designer Frederick Kiesler was director of scenic design at Juilliard from 1933 to 1957.

CHAMBER MUSIC

SOME OF the greatest music ever written was written for chamber music—learning to play with the small group of people that you meet with all the time is one of the best training grounds sociologically on how to behave in a community. When you are in an orchestra, there is the guy waving the baton and yelling at you or encouraging you and inspiring you and you are one of a herd, so to speak—you contribute a lot, but you are not making decisions. But, in chamber music you have to make decisions all the time. **ROBERT MANN**

The Chung Trio rehearsing in 1976. Kyung-Wha Chung, violin; Myung-Wha Chung, cello; and Myung Whun Chung, piano

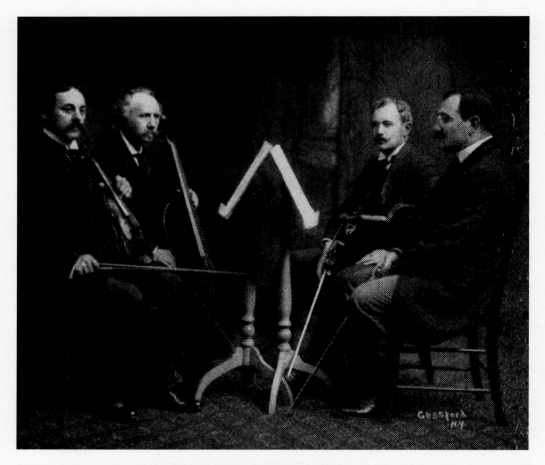

The Kneisel Quartet around the time they came from Boston to join the inaugural string faculty of the Institute of Musical Art. Franz Kneisel (1865–1926) emigrated to the United States from his native Austria in 1885 to assume the position of concertmaster of the Boston Symphony Orchestra. That same year, he formed the Kneisel Quartet, the first professional string quartet in America, which was in existence as an ensemble until 1917. The quartet presented many important premieres during its thirty-two-year lifespan, including the world premiere in Boston of Dvorak's *American Quartet*, in 1894.

Hans Letz coaching a chamber-music group, early 1950s. A German violinist born in 1887, Letz emigrated to the United States in 1908. He appeared as soloist with major ensembles around the country and was second violinist of the Kneisel Quartet from 1912 to 1917. He was a member of Juilliard's faculty from 1912 to 1956.

I REMEMBER getting groups together for all kinds of things. We would go out and play concerts in schools—that was part of the school's goal, and it gave us a chance to perform pieces many times, not just once. We had a very good time. We had a group that did these school concerts with pieces for violin and piano, clarinet and piano, and we always finished with the Bartók *Contrasts*. **JAMES LEVINE**

Clockwise from top left: New York Woodwind Quintet (Carol Wincenc, flute; Ronald Roseman, oboe; Charles Neidich, clarinet; William Purvis, horn; Donald MacCourt, bassoon) with guest artists Ayako Oshima (bass clarinet) and Raymond Mase (trumpet) performing Hindemith's Septett für Blasinstrumente (1948) at the quintet's April 7, 1999 faculty recital

American Brass Quintet recital, February 1, 1999

Percussion Ensemble, led by Daniel Druckman, December 12, 1997. The program was devoted to percussion music from Latin America.

Joseph Fuchs tribute concert in Juilliard Theater, January 18, 1995. Left to right: Stephen Clapp, Dean; Glenn Dicterow; Joseph Fuchs. Fuchs (1899–1997) entered the Institute of Musical Art in 1906 at age seven, studying with Louis Svečenski and Franz Kneisel. Following graduation in 1918, he began a long career that included solo and concerto performances, numerous recordings, and a fourteen-year tenure as concertmaster of the Cleveland Orchestra (1926–40). He taught at Juilliard from 1946 until his death. Stephen Clapp, a member of Juilliard's violin faculty since 1987, was appointed Dean in 1994. He studied with Dorothy DeLay and Ivan Galamian. Glenn Dicterow is the concertmaster of the New York Philharmonic. He has been a member of Juilliard's violin faculty since 1987.

WILLIAM SCHUMAN

William Schuman at work on his Symphony for Strings (Symphony No. 5) in 1943

WILLIAM SCHUMAN, you might say,
is the man who shaped the vision
that became the Juilliard of today.
ROBERT MANN

Leonard Rose, William Schuman, Jean Morel, and
William Bergsma at a special Juilliard Orchestra
concert during the opening week of Philharmonic
Hall, September 28, 1962. The program included
the world premiere of Bergsma's *In Celebration:
Toccata for the Sixth Day* and Schuman's
*A Song of Orpheus: Fantasy for Violoncello and
Orchestra*, with Leonard Rose, cellist.

Above: William Schuman talking to Edith Braun at a reception held after commencement exercises on the school's north terrace, 1959

I THINK William Schuman was an extraordinary individual… he had incredible intuition and insight, and perhaps more importantly, he had the self-confidence to trust that intuition and to act on it. He understood the idea of Juilliard as being half a European conservatory, but also half a new institute for the arts that had to provide new ways of learning, and new ways of thinking about the arts. He was, in that sense, really way, way ahead of his time. **EDWARD BILOUS**

BILL CHANGED the whole nature of the school. Nothing remained the same. Much of the faculty changed, and he brought in something called L & M—Literature and Materials of Music—which was simply a way of teaching theory. He brought in young composers to do the teaching of L & M as well as the teaching of composition. The school began having festivals of contemporary music; he brought in the Juilliard String Quartet. Oh, one can go on and on. **MILTON BABBITT**

IT WAS really Bill Schuman who transformed the institution and made it look toward the future in a very aggressive way. He made it a distinctly American institution. There was an integration of academic studies with performance studies, the idea that the individuals, the young people who went to Juilliard, really had to grow as individuals, as well as artists. **JOSEPH W. POLISI**

Opposite, above: Mark Schubart, dean of The Juilliard School under William Schuman

Opposite, below: Aaron Copland's *Piano Fantasy* was commissioned for Juilliard's fiftieth anniversary and premiered by William Masselos on October 25, 1957. A photocopy of the holograph score is housed in the Juilliard library.

BILL WAS an amazingly creative and innovative person. He was a visionary. In fact, Mark Schubart, who was his dean for all those years, once joked with me. He said,"I was always kidding Bill that I was going to ask him when he was going to start his medical school at Juilliard, since he started so many other things."
JOSEPH W. POLISI

SCHUMAN had the idea that his faculty would be a kind of colony around him. We were a jolly group. **JOSEPH BLOCH**

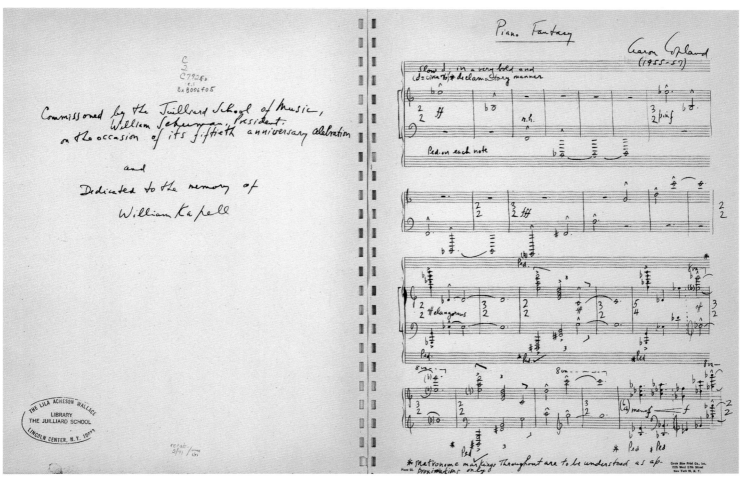

THE JUILLIARD STRING

QUARTET

A PAIR OF PREMIERES

In 2 Special Concerts By

THE JUILLIARD STRING QUARTET

"The very model of modern quartet playing at its best." —The New York Times

New York Premiere April 16th
Vincent Persichetti's Fourth String Quartet
Op. 122 (Parable X)

New York Premiere May 7th
Alberto Ginastera's Third String Quartet
Benita Valente, soprano

**2 Tuesday Evenings
Alice Tully Hall at 8:30
Subscriptions $7**

Above: Program cover, 1973–74. The Juilliard String Quartet was a pioneer in expanding the boundaries of repertory for a string quartet, playing both classical repertoire and premiering new music by contemporary composers.

Left: The Juilliard String Quartet II in 1957. Left to right: Robert Koff, second violin; Robert Mann , first violin; Raphael Hillyer, viola; and, Claus Adam, cello

THE CREATION of the Juilliard String Quartet was a bold stroke. It doesn't sound that innovative today because there are so many wonderful string quartets in residence at various institutions around the country—but, in 1946, this was a big deal. There really weren't that many great American string quartets out there. It was right after the war and there was enormous upheaval and change. To have a professional string quartet in residence at a music school was a new idea. **JOSEPH W. POLISI**

WHEN I WAS a student at Juilliard, one of the influential musicians in the school was a man who was the assistant conductor of the orchestra. His name was Edgar Schenkman, and he was a friend of Schuman's. I said to him, "Don't you think with this new president of Juilliard, William Schuman, that it's about time Juilliard had a resident string quartet?" Edgar Schenkman looked like the Cheshire cat that just swallowed something and said, "I happen to know that's exactly what he has in mind."… The next thing I knew, I was asked for an interview with William Schuman. I didn't know him. He was a very sharp man, very intelligent. I decided I was just going to be myself, I was not going to angle for anything. So, we talked. Interestingly enough, we talked about music. He didn't talk about jobs. He said, "What do you think about this? What do you think about that?" And I said something that later became a kind of slogan— that it was important to play old music as if it had been just written and new music as if it had been around for a long time. He loved it … and that's how the Juilliard quartet began.

ROBERT MANN

Opposite: Juilliard String Quartet (left to right): Claus Adam, cello; Robert Mann, first violin; Raphael Hillyer, viola; and Isidore Cohen, second violin, at McGuire Air Force Base just before their departure for Iceland by military transport, August 23, 1958. The Juilliard Quartet played three concerts in Iceland, then flew to Edinburgh to perform all six Bartók quartets in the Edinburgh Festival. From there, the ten-week tour continued, partly under the auspices of the State Department, to Germany, Greece, Turkey, Hungary, and Poland. They also performed at the Brussels World's Fair and in concerts in Vienna and Paris.

Right: The Juilliard String Quartet, c. 1975 (left to right): Robert Mann, Earl Carlyss, Joel Krosnick, Samuel Rhodes

Above: The current Juilliard String Quartet performing Elliott Carter's String Quartet No. 5, in honor of the composer's ninetieth-birthday celebration, December 14, 1998. In 1997, founding member Robert Mann retired after fifty-one years with the quartet. Joel Smirnoff, for eleven years the group's second violinist, moved into Mann's chair, and Ronald Copes joined the quartet to take Smirnoff's old position.

Right: Composer and Juilliard faculty member Milton Babbitt, standing, with the Juilliard String Quartet (Robert Mann, left, Joel Smirnoff, Joel Krosnick, and Samuel Rhodes) in 1996. The Juilliard String Quartet premiered Babbitt's Quintet for Clarinet and String Quartet with clarinetist Charles Neidich at the Juilliard Theater in October 1996, marking the fiftieth anniversary of the JuilliardString Quartet's first performance.

Juilliard String Quartet first violinist Joel Smirnoff coaching students, c. 1998

EVERY SINGLE person who was involved in the Juilliard String Quartet—that's about ten or eleven people—was hipped on teaching… and there's never been a member of the Juilliard Quartet who didn't want to teach and so… in that sense we were encouraging people wherever we met them to come and study at Juilliard. I can remember very distinctly the beginnings of the Tokyo Quartet; we were in Japan and we'd arranged to teach gifted young Japanese string players…. We got Juilliard to accept them on scholarship and that's how the Tokyo Quartet started. We did that with many quartets. We also helped shape quartets like the Emerson, the American, the Mendelssohn. As a matter of fact, I would say about three-quarters of all the string quartets in America have been taught by members of the Juilliard Quartet. **ROBERT MANN**

PRE-COLLEGE PROGRAM

THE INSTITUTE OF MUSICAL ART PREPARATORY CENTER (LATER THE PRE-COLLEGE DIVISION) OPENED IN 1916 AND OFFERED TRAINING TO YOUNG MUSICIANS. FROM 1921 TO 1924 CHARLES SEEGER AND HIS FIRST WIFE CONSTANCE SEEGER (THE PARENTS OF FOLK SINGER AND POLITICAL ACTIVIST PETE SEEGER) WERE ITS DIRECTORS OF PIANO INSTRUCTION AND VIOLIN INSTRUCTION, RESPECTIVELY.

I PERSONALLY believe the most important thing about the Juilliard School is the pre-college, because that is our future. I am very, very fascinated with what happens to pre-college kids between the ages of twelve and eighteen. There can be someone who is fantastically talented at twelve and a has-been at seventeen, or someone who is just mediocre at twelve and brilliant at seventeen, or someone who has medium talent but works very hard and does so well that he or she becomes a fantastic and wonderful musician. That all happens in the pre-college! **ITZHAK PERLMAN**

Above: Pre-college student Peter Schaaf entering the Claremont Avenue building, c 1952. He writes, "Who knew when my father took that picture, that I would still be intimately involved with the school as a photographer almost fifty years later?"

Left: Young student at work

9/1935

Lily and Helen Miki, daughters of Riokichi Miki, a Japanese artist

CAREERS AHEAD FOR TWO GIRLS

Japanese Youngsters, 9 1-2 and 14, Shine in Music.

WALTER DAMROSCH AIDS THEM

Both Now Have Scholarships at Juilliard School.

ing bar, conducted in a way which is at once gay and refined, despite the fact that it is, in appearance, the nearest thing to the old-fashioned saloon in New York city.

But it takes Miki to finish the success story, as it was he who really began it. Miki, having persuaded the Misses Tucker and Russell that they should serve afternoon tea in their antique shop, landed himself a permanent job with them, and got married. The business grew from an antique shop to a restaurant.

Miki brought in his Japanese friends to serve as chefs and waiters. He occasionally brought in some of his own pictures, which the Misses Tucker and Russell hung for decoration. Out of this grew an art gallery, conducted along with the tea room.

Above: *The Iron Mountain Michigan News*, 1935. From its very inception, the Institute of Musical Art was open to students regardless of race, religion, or country of origin.

Right: America's hometown papers proudly followed the progress and achievements of young people from their communities who attended Juilliard. Articles such as these were pasted by hand into scrapbooks over many decades and are housed in Juilliard's library.

IT'S A LITTLE unnerving when you get on the elevator in the morning with some nine-year-old kid who is better at what he does than you will ever be in your life. **BRADLEY WHITFORD**

Columbus Citizen
4/27/34

GIVES VIOLIN RECITAL

Penelope Johnson, 15-year-old violinist, will give a recital Friday evening in the auditorium of Central High School. With the aid of the funds resulting she will be able to take advantage of a scholarship she has won at the Juilliard School in New York. Penelope lives at 252 S. Hague avenue. She will be graduated from West High School in June.

I DON'T like the word prodigy because it separates these children from the rest of us. What they're doing is just doing everything faster. It's a question of speed. Usually these children have a very strong desire to do the work they're doing. They don't want to watch television; they don't want to go out and play football; they don't want to do these other things—they want to play the violin. And so they drag the parents along with them. **DOROTHY DELAY**

Above: Violinist and pedagogue Dorothy DeLay as a young girl, with her violin and her cousin (on the right)

Right: Pre-College Orchestra students tuning up backstage, May 2001

Below: Pianist and composer Marvin Hamlisch age six, at the time he was enrolled in the Juilliard Preparatory Division

I THINK pressure is a word that is synonymous with Juilliard.... Because you're six, you're seven, you're eight years old. Here's where the pressure comes from. One piece of pressure is simply having heard at home from your parents, "This is a God-given gift—God is the one who gave you this gift. You now must pay back to God." So, you have that going in one ear. You have your teacher saying, "You're really good, but you know, come on, you could be better." Then there's this other world out there called reality—you know? So what happens, finally, is you have certain kids who are wildly talented but cannot take this kind of pressure and will break. You'll have other kids who are wildly talented but unfortunately don't have the desire. Then you have what happens in the real world, which is you have a lot of talented people and a lot of people just don't make it. **MARVIN HAMLISCH**

I REMEMBER going to learn my lines on the fourth floor and just sitting in front of one of those piano rehearsal rooms, which are about six inches longer than the grand piano (you can barely open the door for the student to get in), and just knowing I was hearing something brilliant, that only a couple of people in the world could do that well. I had a huge crush on one woman, a pianist; I was too shy even to talk to her and I always saw her on the weekends ... and I then I found out that she was only fifteen [laughs]. **VAL KILMER**

Above: A young Itzhak Perlman

Below: Violinist Midori, April 1987. Midori studied with Dorothy DeLay at Juilliard.

PRE-COLLEGE for me was phenomenal. I remember it so vividly and with the warmest memories. It's where I established friends that I still have today. I had to come in from Jersey, which I thought was such a schlepp, but then there were people coming in from California. It was incredible. Because it's only one day out of the week, you have to cram everything into that day, which means ear-training, theory, piano, and, of course, there was orchestra, there was your instrument lesson—all of this had to be crammed into one day! **NADJA SALERNO-SONNENBERG**

IT'S HARD to stay on track. I mean you are practicing many, many hours during a time when you want to play outside, you want to go to parties, you want to have friends. You want to do things that normal kids do. And you're playing the piano all day long, getting up, practicing a couple hours before school…after school…going to your teacher's house every single day. It's an abnormal life. There's no doubt about it. **JULIE CHOI**

Clockwise from top right: Piano student Tiffany Huang, c. 1998

Violinist Rachel Lee (seated, center) with her friends from school, spring 2002. Rachel studied with Dorothy DeLay at Juilliard and was featured in the *American Masters* documentary *Juilliard*.

Music Advancement Program (MAP) cello student Jessica Constant, c. 1998

IN THE

IT WAS so wonderful to know that I was in a place where what I wanted to do more than anything in the world was the thing that was valued and nurtured by the faculty. They wanted us to play our instruments as well as we could, and at the same time they provided us with really interesting academic courses. **PAULA ROBISON**

THE IDEA of Literature and Materials of Music was to do away with textbooks, the old counterpoint-theory textbooks. You were supposed to work from the music.... I remember my first day of teaching [piano literature]. Here I was, scared stiff, going into this class of young virtuosi. I sat down and I played a piece of the sixteenth–seventeenth-century English virginal composer, John Bull, and then I turned to the class and said, "What is peculiar about that?" And one of the students said, "You're pedaling." I almost threw myself out of the sixth-floor window. After that, there was no place to go but up. **JOSEPH BLOCH**

CLASSROOM

ONE OF THE GROUNDBREAKING ACADEMIC PROGRAMS INITIATED BY WILLIAM SCHUMAN IN 1947 WAS THE LITERATURE AND MATERIALS OF MUSIC (L & M) PROGRAM, A NEW WAY TO STUDY THEORY THAT REVOLUTIONIZED ACADEMIC STUDY OF THIS SUBJECT. SCHUMAN BELIEVED THAT TO CREATE THE IDEAL ENVIRONMENT FOR LEARNING, THE CURRICULUM ITSELF HAD TO CONNECT WITH THE PERFORMERS' EXPERIENCES AND NEEDS, RELYING ON CREATIVE TEACHER-STUDENT INTERACTION AND WORKING WITH THE MUSIC ITSELF. NO TEXTBOOKS WERE USED; RATHER, THE ELEMENTS OF MUSIC ARE LEARNED THROUGH DIRECT STUDY OF SCORES. IN ADDITION TO TAKING LITERATURE AND MATERIALS OF MUSIC, STUDENTS ARE REQUIRED TO TAKE HISTORY COURSES IN THEIR DISCIPLINE, A SEQUENCE OF LIBERAL ARTS COURSES, AND SPECIAL DEPARTMENTAL COURSES. JUILLIARD STUDENTS TODAY ARE ALSO ENCOURAGED TO PARTICIPATE IN EDUCATIONAL OUTREACH PROGRAMS IN THE COMMUNITY.

Opposite: A member of the piano literature and Literature and Materials of Music (L & M) faculties from 1948 to 1998, pianist Joseph Bloch studied with Olga Samaroff and came to teach at Juilliard at the invitation of William Schuman.

THE JUILLIARD of the twenty-first century provides a curriculum in which our students learn in the concert hall, in the rehearsal room, and in the classroom. We urge our students to view their priorities in a horizontal manner, with classroom studies existing at the same level of importance as all of their performance work. We believe that performance studies combined with nonartistic academic study enriches the development of the total performing artist. **JOSEPH W. POLISI**

I AM ALWAYS interested every time I find a really bright person in their early twenties or thirties who has considered the classical education essential. You can't function without it; without the continuum, you have no way to know what anything is based on—and you're put in the position artistically of reinventing the wheel, which is just ridiculous, when the information is all there.... Only the exceptional ones realize that they can never know too much. **JAMES LEVINE**

I THINK IN every music school the battle rages between people who think their students ought to be spending more time practicing their instruments and the other people who are saying "Oh no, they're already practicing too much ...they don't understand what they're doing...they need to have a broader cultural base." Schuman, as I understand what he envisioned, was trying to create a situation where we would have performers and composers who were aware enough of the great tradition of their instruments and their heritage to be able to make informed choices. People come to Juilliard very centered on practicing their instruments, and many of them believe that by just practicing more and more they'll be able to achieve what they need to achieve.... But, certainly it seems clear that without a real understanding of how the music that they're playing fits into a much larger frame, they can't ever achieve a really good performance! **BRUCE BRUBAKER**

Left, above: The Juilliard Electric Ensemble was created in 2002 to provide students with the opportunity to use new technology in performance. Founded and directed by Edward Bilous (right), chairman of the Literature and Materials Department, the Juilliard Electric Ensemble is the first Juilliard chamber music ensemble to include actors and dancers with musicians in the creation of interdisciplinary works. Violinist Airi Yoshioka (left) and Juilliard Music Technology Center faculty member Milica Paranosic (center) participated in the premiere of the ensemble in June 2002. The Juilliard Electric Ensemble will be featured at Beyond the Machine, a festival of electronic and interactive music at Lincoln Center, and performs on Juilliard InterArts events.

Left, below: From 1980 to 1992, Bruce Brubaker earned three degrees in piano at Juilliard. In 1988, *Musical America* named him a Young Musician of the Year, and, in 1995, he joined the Juilliard faculty. An advocate of music as a component of interdisciplinary performance, he has extended the role of the traditional classical pianist—in his own work and in a new InterArts project at Juilliard. His other projects at Juilliard have included the well-received retrospective of twentieth-century piano music, "Piano Century." Brubaker has performed with the Los Angeles Philharmonic and at Tanglewood, Lincoln Center's Mostly Mozart Festival, and the Hollywood Bowl.

I WOULD organize ensembles on my own. We would do concerts both at Juilliard and around town. I became a director of a youth orchestra, I would work for the ballet, I would accompany dance on the piano. To earn some money, I would play piano for violinists and clarinetists for their juries. I would conduct exercise and breathing classes for the singers. I would do anything I could to immerse myself in the musical world. The academic side I avoided. I just didn't go to class.... Sitting in a classroom, for me, wasn't the way to do it. I would walk out of classes, in some cases. And most of the time I just wouldn't go.... I was doing everything I could on the performance end, not just to avoid going to the other classes, but because that is what I wanted to do. **LEONARD SLATKIN**

Sharon Isbin, founder and chair of the guitar department, with student Adam Brown, 2002

JUILLIARD HAS A LONG TRADITION OF EDUCATIONAL PROGRAMS THAT SERVE THE BROADER COMMUNITY. THE SUMMER SCHOOL PROGRAM, WHICH EXISTED FROM 1932 TO 1952, OFFERED INDIVIDUAL INSTRUCTION IN INSTRUMENTS AND VOICE AS WELL AS CLASSES IN THEORY, EAR TRAINING, AND PUBLIC-SCHOOL MUSIC TEACHING. THEORIST GEORGE A. WEDGE WAS DIRECTOR OF THE SUMMER SCHOOL PROGRAM FROM 1932 TO 1948. FACULTY MEMBERS WERE DRAWN FROM THOSE OF THE INSTITUTE OF MUSICAL ART AND JUILLIARD GRADUATE SCHOOL AND INCLUDED MANY PROMINENT PERFORMERS. JUILLIARD'S PRESENT EVENING DIVISION PROGRAM BEGAN IN 1946 AS THE EXTENSION DEPARTMENT. THE EVENING DIVISION CURRENTLY OFFERS BETWEEN FIFTY TO SIXTY CREDIT AND NONCREDIT COURSES TO MORE THAN SIXTEEN HUNDRED STUDENTS EACH YEAR.

Above: Summer school 1932, group instruction in piano

Opposite, above: Among the offerings of the Evening Division is the Juilliard Choral Union, a community-based symphonic chorus directed by Judith Clurman. The Choral Union presents performances on its own and in conjunction with Juilliard's large ensembles. On April 5, 2002, Judith Clurman led the Juilliard Choral Union and Orchestra in a performance of Beethoven's Mass in C Major, Op. 86, at Alice Tully Hall. The program also included the likely U.S. premiere of a Wagner student work, an unaccompanied choral fugue titled "Dein ist das Reich von Ewigkeit zu Ewigkeit."

Opposite, below: Carl Friedberg teaching summer school, 1950. A young piano student, Van Cliburn, can be seen in the fourth row, third from the right.

SOLOISTS

VAN CLIBURN was a very important figure—just the fact of Van Cliburn, in 1958, winning the Tchaikovsky Competition and having a ticker-tape parade…and being this person with a great sense of public relations…. He became an icon, and encouraged young American males to study the piano. Before that time, the American male pianist was considered kind of offbeat, not really an acceptable profession. But Van Cliburn and what followed made it respectable.

I'm famous because I flunked Van Cliburn! From the moment he came to Juilliard he was under management and toured constantly. I would leave my house to drive in at eight o'clock in the morning and the phone would ring at eight-fifteen and Van would say, "Mrs Bloch, this is Van. I'm so sorry. I just got back from touring and I'm so tired. Would you tell Mr. Bloch I'm tired." He was a sweetheart. He still is. But he didn't show up very often. So, I had to give him insufficient attendance.

JOSEPH BLOCH

'How Does It Feel?'—Van Cliburn Expresses It in Many Ways From Lower Broadway to the Keyboard

The New York Times (by Neal Boenzi)

The 23-year-old pianist who conquered Moscow had another triumph here yesterday. This is how he reacted in traditional ticker-tape parade, and as he played at Waldorf luncheon.

Opposite: Pianist and piano pedagogue Rosina Lhévinne with star pupil Van Cliburn

Above: The New York Times, May 21, 1958, featuring photographs of Van Cliburn at the ticker-tape parade that celebrated his return to America after his historic triumph in Moscow, where he won the Tchaikovsky Piano Competition

Left: Considered one of today's finest interpreters of the music of Frederic Chopin, pianist Garrick Ohlsson is also noted for his virtuosic performances of the works of Mozart, Beethoven, and Schubert. Born in White Plains, New York, he enrolled at Juilliard at the age of thirteen and studied with Sascha Gorodnitzki and Rosina Lhévinne. At age twenty-one, he was the first American to win the Chopin International Piano Competition in Warsaw, and he went on to win first prizes at the 1966 Busoni Competition in Italy and the 1968 Montreal Piano Competition. Today, Ohlsson plays concerts throughout the world.

Opposite: Pinchas Zukerman, violinist, violist, conductor, teacher, chamber musician, and exponent of contemporary music, was born in Tel Aviv, Israel in 1948. He began musical training with his father, first on recorder, then clarinet, and ultimately violin. He came to America in 1962 to study with Ivan Galamian at Juilliard. In 1967, after winning First Prize in the twenty-fifth Leventritt International Competition, Mr. Zukerman began his solo career. Mr. Zukerman's conducting career began in 1970 with the English Chamber Orchestra, and he has conducted many of the world's leading orchestras. He presents master classes and young people's concert performances to educate future classical musicians and audiences. Mr. Zukerman is currently music director of the National Arts Centre Orchestra in Ottawa, Ontario.

AT AGE twenty, I had no question in my mind that a big solo career was beckoning and that would be my life. It was going to start right away.... I mean, there was no question that it would. It wasn't going to take twenty years to develop. I suppose, to a certain extent, that belief traces back to the Cliburn story and that, even in the 1970s, people were still believing that an American could spring forth fully formed and capture the attention of the world—as a pianist! I don't think the realities of how difficult that might be were at all apparent to me or to anybody else. **BRUCE BRUBAKER**

Simon Estes in the title role of Verdi's *Simon Boccanegra,* performed by the Washington Opera Company at the Kennedy Center, 1998

Boris

Above: Violinist Nadja Salerno-Sonnenberg studied with Dorothy DeLay in Juilliard's Pre-College Division and went on to win the prestigious Walter W. Naumberg International Violin Competition in 1981. She broke the mold as a classical musician with her appearances on the *Tonight Show* and as the subject of major television programs and films. Her high profile has made her a celebrity not just in musical circles but also with the general public.

WHEN I went to school, if one out of a hundred kids was successful as a soloist, that was amazing. And I'm telling you it's much less now. It depends on your instrument. A trombone player is not going to Juilliard to be a soloist. But every pianist? You can be sure. And every violinist? Oh, you bet.... To learn how to play their instrument so that they could be in a quartet? It's an option, and it may be the first option for some players. But when I went to school, I didn't know anybody who wanted that.

NADJA SALERNO-SONNENBERG

Right: John Browning began to study the piano at age five and gave his first public performance as a soloist with the Denver Symphony at age ten. He moved to New York to study on scholarship with Rosina Lhévinne at Juilliard. He won the Steinway Centennial Award in 1954, the Leventritt Competition in 1955, and placed second at the Queen Elisabeth International Music Competition in Brussels in 1956. That same year he made his professional concerto debut with the New York Philharmonic under Dmitri Mitropoulos. He has been closely associated with the music of Samuel Barber, and presented the world premiere of the composer's Concerto for Piano and Orchestra with the Boston Symphony Orchestra under Erich Leinsdorf in 1962.

ONE OF the things that influenced me was that the life of a soloist is lonely. For performing artists, balancing home and continuous travel is a very difficult thing to come to terms with. Some people do it with fantastic grace and apparent ease. And other people are never completely comfortable with it.
JAMES LEVINE

Above: Itzhak Perlman, New York, 1973

Below: Yo-Yo Ma at a rehearsal of the New York Philharmonic Orchestra with Zubin Mehta conducting, in Avery Fisher Hall, December 1980. Yo-Yo Ma studied with Leonard Rose in Juilliard's Pre-College Division from 1964 to 1971.

DANCE

THERE HAD never been a dance division associated with a conservatory. It was really out of whole cloth and Bill Schuman's vision that the whole thing started. He believed very strongly that dance and music belong together. **MURIEL TOPAZ**

Faculty review at The Juilliard School, spring 2000

THE EARLIEST modern dance was in revolt against the classical dance, against ballet, and therefore putting them under one roof and having dancers study both techniques was a very controversial move. You were either in the modern dance camp or the ballet camp—the camps didn't cross.... Martha Hill had danced with Martha Graham and she had started the Bennington Dance Festival, which was a very important milestone in the history of American dance—It was the place where American modern dance really came of age. She had a lot of friends in the dance world and people trusted her judgment because she'd created something that was very important. **MURIEL TOPAZ**

THERE WAS no synthesis at that time between ballet and modern. The ballet people thought the modern people were just weird and ugly, and the moderns thought the ballets were decorative and effete. That's the way dance was [then]. How Martha Hill got them to agree to be in the same spaces at the same time was amazing. For those of us who were going to get the rewards of that, it was incredible. **BRUCE MARKS**

Opposite: Martha Hill dancing on the tennis court at Bennington College, c. 1935

Above: Juilliard dancers in rehearsal for *Night,* a work by dancer, choreographer, and Juilliard faculty member Anna Sokolow, May 1966

MARTHA HILL was an anomaly in ways. I mean she seemed like she should be running bridge parties in the suburbs, and yet, here she was, placating and getting work and choreography out of three or four of the most interesting choreographers in the history of dance. And she managed somehow to keep these people working and not choking each other to death. It was quite amazing how she juggled all of these very big people, these huge egos, and kept them all there and working and dedicated to Juilliard. **BRUCE MARKS**

Martha Hill with her husband, Thurston Davies, c. 1958

MARTHA HILL was wonderful looking. She wore very high stacked heels and a bun on the side of her head. She walked terribly erect as though there was a rod up her back, and she had a rather strident voice. She had incredible energy and she was very hands-on as the director of the department. She would have been a wonderful character in a Bette Davis film. She had large eyes and a round face. She was quite beautiful, striking in a way. Even when I saw her many years after I graduated, she hadn't aged at all. **MARTHA CLARKE**

Martha Hill, with her back turned, signature bun in view, on a rehearsal stage with dancer Terese Capucilli, who is now on the faculty at Juilliard

IT WAS fantastic how Martha Hill took care of each student. The way she watched them and helped them. If they had a problem they could go to her and tell her…. She also went to every concert—till she was old…she saw everything…. She took care and paid attention to what people were doing. **PINA BAUSCH**

MARTHA HILL was an eminent educator who somehow had talked all of these great forces into coming together at this school at this time … José Limón, Antony Tudor, Margaret Craske—the great Cecchetti expert—Martha Graham, Doris Humphrey and her counterpart at the Graham School, Louis Horst. They were all there. **BRUCE MARKS**

Left to right: Martha Hill, Doris Humphrey, and Louis Horst, 1958

Dancer and choreographer, Martha Clarke (right), when she was a student at The Juilliard School, mid-1960s

YOU COULDN'T have chosen bigger stars in the field to study with than Juilliard offered at the time. That's why I went there. **MARTHA CLARKE**

Opposite: José Limón, 1965

Above: Muriel Topaz and Antony Tudor observing in a dance studio at Juilliard. Muriel "Micki" Topaz had been a dance student at Juilliard from 1951 to 1954; afterward, she became a member of the dance faculty and, ultimately, followed Martha Hill as director of the division, from 1985 to 1992.

THE DANCE Department was glamorous because every important person in the dance world was on the faculty. You would go into the cafeteria up at Claremont Avenue and see Martha Graham standing in the cafeteria line holding a red rose while she got the fish.
JOSEPH BLOCH

Above: Margaret Craske, the quintessential teacher of ballet technique, at Juilliard, c. 1960. Craske believed that technique was only a small part of what made the dancer; she did not believe in fads or fashion but in truth and simplicity in dance.

Opposite: Martha Graham joined Juilliard's dance faculty when the division was founded in 1951, and she taught at the school until 1977. In April 1952, her company presented a special series of performances at Juilliard, including the premiere performance of *Canticle for Innocent Comedians* (music by Thomas Ribbink), which was commissioned by the School. The series also included her work *Judith*, with music by William Schuman, and the New York premiere of *The Triumph of Saint Joan,* with music by Norman Dello Joio.

ANY QUESTION I had about dance history, they were all there. You know, I was living it. It was just an extraordinary time. We studied composition; we had Literature and Materials of Music, and anatomy. These were areas of exploration that I had never had. **BONNIE ODA HOMSEY**

Left: Alfredo Corvino, ballet instructor at Juilliard, 1976

Below: Dance Division anatomy class, 1962

Opposite, above: Bessie Schonberg seated with Juilliard students, c. 1996. Ms. Schonberg was born in Hanover, Germany, to an American opera singer who worked in Europe before World War I. After the war, she attended the University of Oregon in Eugene, where she met dance teacher Martha Hill, who encouraged her to move to New York in 1929. There she studied with Martha Graham and performed briefly with Graham's company until, in 1931, an injury forced her to curtail her performing career. She taught dance composition at Juilliard from 1992 until her death in 1997. Her renown as one of America's most influential teachers of dance composition and a mentor to dancers was recognized by the creation, in 1984, of the "Bessie" performance awards by the Dance Theater Workshop. In 1988, Ms. Schonberg herself was honored with a Bessie for her lifetime service to dance.

Opposite, below: Kazuko Hirabayashi, a member of the dance faculty at Juilliard, 1979

Above: Benjamin Harkarvy, artistic director of the Juilliard dance division from 1990 to 2002, teaching a class at Pennsylvania Ballet Company, c. 1970s

Left: Bruce Marks

Opposite, above: Benjamin Harkarvy, 2002

Opposite, below: Benjamin Harkarvy with his students, c. 1996

Overleaf: Dancers in a performance of José Limón's *The Winged,* with a score by Juilliard student composer Jon Magnussen, Spring Dance Recital, 1996

THIS WONDERFUL thing happens in New York—all the dancers rush to a certain teacher. Everyone in the world is looking for a guru. I remember in the 1950s, we all ran to a young man named Benjamin Harkarvy, who was teaching at Dance Players, a studio in Manhattan. The classes were really interesting and he explained beautifully the substance of the work. Ben went on to work at Pennsylvania Ballet, and he went to Holland, where he worked with the great Dutch choreographers who, in their own way, were involved in the synthesis of modern dance and ballet in the company called Netherlands Dance Theatre. It was so logical for him to be at Juilliard, because his directing and training went that way…that kind of coalescing of modern dance and ballet that he so believed in, and that is so right for our time. **BRUCE MARKS**

THE MOVE TO
LINCOLN CENTER

THE CREATION of Lincoln Center for the Performing Arts was a very powerful, artistic and financial concept—backed up by some of the most prominent financiers and philanthropists in New York City and, therefore, the United States—to bring together the Metropolitan Opera and the New York Philharmonic and perhaps create new constituents that would be involved in the performing arts in New York City. From the very beginning, the concept of some type of educational venture at Lincoln Center was always there, but the question was, should the founding fathers of Lincoln Center create an absolutely new educational venture, or find something that already existed? This is where William Schuman comes in, because Bill was a visionary, and he really had a sense of what the future could be and how to achieve it. Bill always said that the school of the arts located at Lincoln Center would be the leading school in the United States, because of the complementary forces that he felt would exist at Lincoln Center. Through the members of his Juilliard board, one or two of whom were also close to John D. Rockefeller III, he began a process of negotiation and persuasion to have the Juilliard School of Music be the educational entity that would be located at this new Lincoln Center for the Performing Arts. **JOSEPH W. POLISI**

Previous pages and above: The Lincoln Center groundbreaking ceremony, May 14, 1959. President Eisenhower, (above) with a symbolic spadeful of dirt, was joined by (left to right) John D. Rockefeller III, president of Lincoln Center for the Performing Arts; David H. Keiser, Robert Moses, chairman of the Mayor's Slum Clearance Committee; Hulan Jack, Manhattan borough president; Mayor Robert Wagner; and New York lieutenant governor Malcolm Wilson.

Opposite: The future site of Lincoln Center on Manhattan's Upper West Side, 1957

THERE WAS a time when Schuman really represented a pinnacle of what American music and American culture was about. He was filled with pride, he was well loved, he was well respected, and he was a very eloquent spokesman. He certainly was ambitious and had very clear ideas about what the American cultural scene should be. When Lincoln Center came into being, he was a natural choice to be the spokesman for that organization, and I think that what he did [resigning as president of Juilliard to become president of Lincoln Center] for Juilliard was to position it as the monument on the hill. Juilliard became more than a music school; it became the place where people would turn, whenever they thought of any issues in arts education…and Juilliard has willingly taken up that mantle. **EDWARD BILOUS**

Below: William Schuman at the construction site of the Metropolitan Opera House at Lincoln Center, c. 1964. As president of The Juilliard School of Music, Schuman was instrumental in Juilliard's selection as the educational constituent of Lincoln Center in February of 1957. In 1961, Schuman resigned his position as president of the Juilliard School of Music to become president of Lincoln Center for the Performing Arts, Inc.

THE PROBLEM with Juilliard is that essentially it is a school…but it is situated at Lincoln Center. That immediately puts them up against the wall. They are part of the whole competitive complex. To protect the young people is a very important, very serious matter. **FRANK CORSARO**

THERE'S NO air in the building.… You can't breathe! None of the windows open. I remember thinking when I first got there, "I'm breathing the same air as Patty LuPone! I'm breathing the same air as Kevin Kline! I'm breathing the same air as David Ogden Stiers!… I'm breathing this wonderful air!" And then by the third year, you're like, "I'm breathing the *same* air! I mean—aaahhh—they need people to open those windows. **LAURA LINNEY**

Right: A view of The Juilliard School building looking southwest, showing the Broadway entrance. The primary architect of the building was Pietro Belluschi and the associate architects, Helge Westermann and Eduardo Catalano.

Below: Visible are the elegant signature gold letters etched in white stone, spelling out the name of the school. Just the sight of those letters have caused more than one heart to skip a beat upon arrival at this corner.

I HAD NEVER been to New York before, and I remember getting in a cab at JFK and asking the driver to go to 66th and Broadway. I remember slinking down in the back of the cab, so that the cab driver could not see me in the rear-view mirror because I had been told all these stories: "You'll be taken for a ride… you'll get taken to New Jersey!" So I'm slinking down, looking up at all the buildings and being amazed and slightly terrified and fascinated by New York City as it sort of blew by me. Then we drove up right to the corner of Juilliard and I looked out the window and there was this granite building with the gold letters "The Juilliard School," and I think I started to weep in the backseat and I completely blew my cover of being, like, some New Yorker, but I was so moved and excited and amazed that I had made it to this place that I had heard so much about. **KEVIN SPACEY**

Above: Lincoln Kirstein and George Balanchine in a School of American Ballet studio at The Juilliard School at Lincoln Center, c. 1970s

THE DANCE Division people were very involved with the plans for the building at Lincoln Center. We met with architects, we were polled about what our needs were, and we expected, as a faculty, to move into six studios. Apparently, at the same time, Peter Mennin was also negotiating with the School of American Ballet, and, as I understand it, his goal was to have the School of American Ballet either replace the Dance Division or at least replace the ballet end of the Dance Division. That plan never came to fruition because I think that Balanchine saw no reason to be under Peter Mennin's thumb. But for many years the School of American Ballet occupied four of the six studios, and obviously that made the Dance Division faculty extremely unhappy. There was no question that there was antipathy and hostility straight along.... It was a most unfortunate period in the history of the school.... How Martha Hill managed not to actually give up the Dance Division, I don't know...she just hung in there by her teeth. **MURIEL TOPAZ**

RE: SAB STUDIOS

4/27/8?

~ ~ ~ ~ ~ ~ ~ ~ ~

We are lucky and grateful to be able to use SAB studios after 7 pm on weeknights. Please keep in mind: if we abuse this priviledge, it will be taken away from us.

PLEASE - no tap dancing ever in any SAB studio. Tapping is only allowed in St. 314.

Thank you

WHEN I ARRIVED at Juilliard in 1984 I remember saying to someone, "What's that glass wall over there on the third floor?" and I was told, "That's the entrance to the School of American Ballet." There were no collaborative programs; we were friendly, but the programs represented two different dance aesthetics. In 1990, when the Rose Building was built at Lincoln Center, the School of American Ballet finally moved to its own studios and the Juilliard Dance Division at Juilliard took over all of these studios. **JOSEPH W. POLISI**

Above: A classic hallway bulletin-board posting reflecting the saga

Right: The tensions between the School of American Ballet and the Juilliard Dance Division, begun in the mid-1960s, continued for more than twenty years, as the two groups battled for space and had to make continual accommodations to each other.

Far right: *The New York Times*, Tuesday, November 2, 1965. Peter Mennin, president of The Juilliard School, reached out to George Balanchine and Lincoln Kirstein of the School of American Ballet, inviting them to be associated with The Juilliard School and be housed in the new Juilliard building at Lincoln Center. This posed a potential threat to the existing Dance Division under the direction of Martha Hill, most notably jeopardizing the ballet program led by Antony Tudor and Margaret Craske. Tudor's roots were in the British school of ballet training, whereas Balanchine, who by this time was one of the most distinguished members of the dance world, came out of the Russian school, which was then influential in the formal training of dancers in America at that time.

THE JUILLIARD SCHOOL

INTER-OFFICE MEMORANDUM

To: All Students   Date: December 22, 1981

From: Dance Division

Subject: S.A.B. Studios

The following stipulations must be strictly followed to insure that we will be allowed by S.A.B. to use their studios for the rest of the year.

1. NO ONE who is not a currently registered Juilliard dance division student is allowed past those glass doors for any reason whatsoever. No exceptions including family or friends even to watch rehearsal. Breaking this rule could result in losing the use of the studios for the rest of the year.

2. The glass doors are to be kept LOCKED at all times. This means having someone come out and lock the door behind you if you leave a rehearsal earlier than is signed up for. We could lose the studios if this is not done.

3. If you cannot use the space you signed up for erase your name to free the space for someone else.

4. No eating, drinking or smoking in the studios.

SCHOOL OF BALLET TO JOIN JUILLIARD

Kirstein-Balanchine Classes to Be at Lincoln Center

The School of American Ballet, the most distinguished school of classic ballet in the country, will become associated with the Juilliard School of Music.

The announcement was made yesterday by Dr. Peter Mennin, president of Juilliard, and George Balanchine and Lincoln Kirstein, heads of the ballet school. The association will start in the fall of 1967, when Juilliard assumes its new function as the educational arm of Lincoln Center for the Performing Arts.

The new association is a further step by Juilliard to serve other performing arts. Juilliard has already announced the formation of a drama division, and also the Juilliard American Opera Center for Advanced Training, both to be inaugurated when the school moves to Lincoln Center.

The School of American Ballet will move from 2291 Broadway when the new Juilliard building at Lincoln Center is completed. There it will establish working relationships with the various existing and future divisions of Juilliard, and also make extensive use of the school's new rehearsal and performance facilities.

The School of American Ballet will remain an independent unit within the Juilliard framework, and will continue to control its own activities. It will be known as the School of American Ballet at Juilliard.

Foundation for Companies

The School of American Ballet, one of the largest in the country, was founded in 1933 when Mr. Kirstein and Edward N. M. Warburg invited Mr. Balanchine and Vladimir Dimitriev to come to the United States to form a school to be based upon the principals of the Russian state ballet academies.

The school became the primary source for all the various companies subsequently founded by Mr. Kirstein and Mr. Balanchine: the American Ballet, Ballet Caravan, Ballet Society and the New York City Ballet, the School of American Ballet being the company's official school.

The faculty of the school, which is headed by Mr. Balanchine, has always employed teachers who were themselves distinguished performing artists. Among these have been Fella Dubrovska and Pierre Vladimiroff, while many of today's outstanding dancers also serve on the faculty. Recently, Diana Adams, a former ballerina of the New York City Ballet, joined the school as its coordinator of studies.

In December, 1963, the School of American Ballet received a grant from the Ford Foundation to strengthen it as a national ballet training institute and to implement a program of assistance to professional ballet training throughout the country.

Advantages Seen

For the School of American Ballet the move to Juilliard offers a number of advantages. Financially, there will probably be little difference, but the conditions in the new building will be incomparably superior.

There is also the hope that one day it will be possible to provide dormitory accommodations, which would bring the school in line with other great state academies of dance.

In addition, in the move to

PETER MENNIN

Peter Mennin in 1945. Mennin was the first-prize winner in the George Gershwin Memorial Contest for Short Symphonic Works for Composers under Thirty Years of Age. Mennin, only twenty-one years old and a veteran of the Army Air Force, heard his work *Symphonic Allegro* performed in public for the first time by the New York Philharmonic, with Leonard Bernstein conducting, at the Metropolitan Opera House. By the time Mennin became president of the Juilliard School in 1962, he was thirty-nine years old and a widely recognized composer of six symphonies and numerous other works.

AT JUILLIARD, the objective of the curriculum has been to combine *breadth* with *depth*. There is no doubt that this presents the best of possible worlds. However, it is also true that it is impossible to accomplish this during the short period of your life that you are under the guidance of the school. That is why the real objective of education remains to teach you how to learn, so that, ideally, your education becomes a continuing process for the rest of your life. **PETER MENNIN**

IN PETER'S eyes, Juilliard was to be a professional performance school on the highest level, and I think it got to that level. Internationally, the great majority of all competitions and prizes were won by Juilliard students. Some people criticize the idea of the school being so competitive, but the professional field is very competitive, and early on it's important that you learn that. Peter's Juilliard was for deeply committed, highly talented people who needed to spend their student years concentrating on honing their talents to the highest possible point. **GEORGANNE MENNIN**

Left: William Schuman greets his successor Peter Mennin at the Lotos Club, November 5, 1962. Mennin assumed the presidency of Juilliard at a time of extraordinary opportunity. Juilliard was now center stage as the educational arm of Lincoln Center, which was considered the heart of cultural life in New York City and, many would say, the world.

Opposite: The fifth president of The Juilliard School, Peter Mennin served for twenty-one years. He was a key figure in the challenging transition from Claremont Avenue to Lincoln Center. It was during his tenure that the Drama Division, the American Opera Center, and the special programs for Young Conductors and Young Playwrights were established. Mennin also developed the Visiting Artists Program, in 1971, and the Festival of Contemporary Music, in 1976. The faculty was "the heart of the school," according to Mennin, and many great artists and teachers came to Juilliard at his invitation. Mennin died in 1983, while actively presiding over school business.

FROM MY point of view, the main contribution of Peter Mennin was to develop a composition department that was so broad.… You really could have contact with practically the whole range of American music at that time.… As Americans, one of the things that we've absorbed is this democratic notion that you and I might disagree, but we can still be in the same family. I think the fact that Bill Schuman and Peter Mennin were creative musicians lends itself to the notion that instead of, "Let's find out the only way to do it and teach that," it was, "Let's open the doors and let the students see the range of things." And the notion that there are different ways to do something and that each person brings something special to the table is probably an American point of view. But it's very persuasive, I think, in the arts. **ELLEN TAAFFE ZWILICH**

COMPOSITION

Composers gathered at Juilliard for the Festival of Contemporary Music, 1981. Seated: President Peter Mennin, Marga Richter. Standing, left to right: Ronald Caltabiano, Milton Babbitt, Eric Ewazen, David Diamond, Benjamin Lees, Lester Trimble, Francis Thorne, and Vincent Persichetti

PEOPLE HAVE this impression that Juilliard, until recently, has not been very interested in new music, and that a lot of the performers who come out of Juilliard have been primarily focused on the traditional repertoire—the old music…. But, there were always a few people who were passionately committed to new music, and there were composers working at Juilliard—not only teaching composition but also teaching L&M [Literature and Materials of Music] who were the most important composers of their time! I mean you had Luciano Berio, Elliott Carter, and Milton Babbitt, all kinds of really important people. Now, there's John Corigliano and Christopher Rouse…. So, at the same time, in the same building, you had performers who were primarily focused on the past and you had people who were only focused on the present and the future! **BRUCE BRUBAKER**

Left: President William Schuman with composers at Juilliard, c. 1958. Seated, left to right: Douglas Moore and Roger Sessions. Standing, left to right: Aaron Copland, Elliott Carter, Wallingford Riegger, William Schuman, and Walter Piston

Right: When Russian composers visited Juilliard on November 17, 1959, a reception was held at the Persian Room of the Plaza Hotel, and a luncheon for the guests at Claremont Avenue. At the luncheon were (left to right) Tikhon Khrennikov, Konstantin Dankevich, President William Schuman, Rosina Lhévinne, and Dr. Boris Yarustovsky. Not pictured but part of the visiting party were Dmitri Shostakovich and Dmitri Kabalevsky. During their visit, the composers attended a rehearsal of the Juilliard Orchestra and heard recorded and live performances of works by Juilliard faculty and alumni.

WHEN I WAS at Juilliard, Vincent Persichetti was the head of the department. Elliott Carter was there. David Diamond, Milton Babbitt, and Roger Sessions were there. It really is kind of a pantheon of American composition, and not just the glittering stars of one kind of music, but quite a range of ideas about how music might be written among those five faculty members.

ELLEN TAAFFE ZWILICH

Roger Sessions (1896–1985) was a member of the Juilliard composition faculty from 1965 to 1983. He attended Harvard at age fourteen and afterward lived in Europe until 1933, when he took a post at Princeton University where he taught for nearly fifty years. Influenced by Stravinsky and Schoenberg, Sessions's earliest scores were in the chromatic post-Romantic style that prevailed in America early in the century. He ultimately incorporated the twelve-tone method into his work. The greater part of his music was written when he was between the ages of fifty and seventy-five, including six of his nine symphonies, the string quintet, the second and third piano sonatas, and his opera *Montezuma*, which was first performed in New York by the American Opera Center at Juilliard in 1982. At Juilliard, he composed some of his most important works, notably *When Lilacs Last in the Dooryard Bloom'd*, based on the Walt Whitman poem. For his last completed piece, Concerto for Orchestra, he was awarded the Pulitzer Prize. Among Sessions's students were Milton Babbitt, Leon Kirchner, David Diamond, Andrew Imbrie, Ralph Shapey, Eric Salzman, Edward Cone, Earl Kim, and Ellen Taaffe Zwilich.

Above left: Born in New York City in 1908, composer Elliott Carter came to Juilliard during the Peter Mennin era, teaching composition from 1966 to 1984. Charles Ives, Walter Piston, and Nadia Boulanger were influential in Carter's development. Considered among the greatest of American composers, Carter has been the recipient of many honors, including the Gold Medal for Music awarded by the National Institute of Arts and Letters, the National Medal of Arts, membership in the American Academy of Arts and Letters and the American Academy of Arts and Sciences, and two Pulitzer Prizes. Carter created a distinctive and innovative nontonal musical language that explored alternatives to rigorous twelve-tone organization. He insisted his students be well versed in the music of the past in order to create a new music for the future.

Above right: Elliott Carter's *String Quartet No. 3* was commissioned by Juilliard for the Juilliard String Quartet. The work was awarded the Pulitzer Prize for Music in 1973. The score is published by Associated Music Publishers.

THE MUSIC of Elliott Carter has raised the standard, raised the bar, so to speak, of demands on performers, more than any other composer in the twentieth century. Works of his that were at first thought unplayable, now pose challenges for every young ensemble throughout the world. To play one of Carter's string quartets is really a way of announcing the mastery of your instrument or your mastery of the literature. For an ensemble to do his Double Concerto or any number of his works is a very powerful statement. **EDWARD BILOUS**

Right: Composer David Diamond was born in 1915 in Rochester, New York. He attended the Cleveland Institute of Music and the Eastman School of Music, where he studied with Bernard Rogers. He later studied with Roger Sessions and Paul Boepple in New York, and with Nadia Boulanger in France. His large catalog of works includes eleven symphonies and numerous other orchestral works, songs, solo instrumental and chamber works. His music employs a range of harmonic styles, with careful attention to formal structural procedures. Diamond was a member of Juilliard's faculty from 1973 to 1997. His Concerto for String Quartet and Orchestra (1994–95) was commissioned by Juilliard for the fiftieth anniversary of the Juilliard String Quartet. A renewed interest in his music in the 1980s was sparked by conductor and former Juilliard student Gerard Schwarz, and, in 1986, Diamond received the William Schuman Lifetime Achievement Award. In 1991, he was awarded the Gold Medal of the American Academy of Arts and Letters and the Edward MacDowell Gold Medal for Lifetime Achievement. In 1995, he was a recipient of the National Medal of Arts.

Left: Vincent Persichetti joined the Juilliard faculty in 1947 and in 1963 was named the chairman of the composition department. In 1970, he became chairman of the Literature and Materials of Music department, and he remained an important and active composer, writer, and teacher until his death in 1987. Born in 1915, in Philadelphia, he began his musical studies at the age of five with piano, organ, double bass, and theory and composition. He later studied piano at the Curtis Institute of Music with Olga Samaroff, who also taught piano at Juilliard. His works combine classicism, romanticism, and modernism—and are both an expression of "high" culture and popular taste.

Left: John Corigliano joined the faculty at Juilliard in 1991. After acclaim for his Symphony No. 1, a response to the AIDS crisis, Corigliano won the 2001 Pulitzer Prize in Music for his Symphony No. 2. Part of the new breed of accomplished American composers, he has received commissions and awards from around the world. His works are admired both for their technique and their expressive nature. Born in New York in 1938, Corigliano comes from a musical family—his father was concertmaster of the New York Philharmonic from 1943 to 1966 and his mother is an accomplished pianist. The Metropolitan Opera commissioned him to write an original opera, *The Ghosts of Versailles*, which premiered in 1991 to sold-out houses. In 1987, he was nominated for an Academy Award for his score for the film *Altered States*, and, in 2000, he received an Academy Award for his score for *The Red Violin*. In 1991, he was elected to the American Academy and Institute of Arts and Letters, and, in 1992, *Musical America* named him their first Composer of the Year.

Opposite: Luciano Berio has been a vital force in the research and development of electronic music and a catalyst in bringing together musicians and computer scientists to investigate new paths for musical composition. In 1950, the Italian-born composer married American singer Cathy Berberian, and many of his vocal pieces were written for her. From 1965 to 1971, Berio was a member of the composition faculty at Juilliard. One former student, Dennis Russell Davies, conducted the world premiere of Berio's *Opera* in 1970. Composer Steve Reich, another former Juilliard student, studied with Berio in California. Among Berio's works is his series of virtuoso pieces for solo instruments, titled *Sequenzas*. Berio collaborated with writer Italo Calvino on two musical works for the stage. As a working composer, he ran the influential electro-acoustic department of IRCAM in Paris until 1980.

Left: At his eighty-fifth birthday celebration, May 7, 2001, Milton Babbitt (center) stands with (from left to right) Robert Mann, Joseph W. Polisi, and Robert Beaser, current chair of the composition faculty.

CONDUCTING

Kurt Masur conducting the Juilliard
Orchestra at Avery Fisher Hall,
February 23, 1998

JEAN MOREL was brought by William Schuman to the school. He saw an extraordinary talent, somebody who could do pretty much what nobody else could do, and that was teach conducting. It's one thing to be able to pick up an instrument and be able to demonstrate to your students what an instrument can do, but it's another, to be able to actually teach conducting. There are very few who can do it. But Morel was one of them. **LEONARD SLATKIN**

I KNEW I'd found what I really wanted to do…and in Morel's class I could tell that he responded to something in my talents that caused him to encourage me. I think I was pretty much full steam ahead about conducting when I got there. But I was also very aware that I would need the piano as a coaching tool. It was my father who convinced me that I would want the piano in order to play song recitals, to play chamber pieces, and once in a while maybe to play a Mozart piano concerto.… I had the good fortune to be able to develop what my best talents were—and that coincided with what I most wanted to do. That is extraordinary luck. **JAMES LEVINE**

Jean Morel, conductor and faculty member at Juilliard from 1948 to 1971, in rehearsal for *The Mines of Sulphur*, an opera in three acts by Richard Rodney Bennett. Composed in 1963, the opera is written in a musical language that makes use of twelve-tone techniques. It was given its U.S. premiere at Juilliard in 1968.

Above: Joel Sachs conducting the New Juilliard Ensemble in the opening concert of the 1998 FOCUS! Festival *Scandinavia Today*, January 23, 1998, Alice Tully Hall

Right: The Juilliard Orchestra in rehearsal with Edgar Schenkman conducting, 1940s

Opposite: Leonard Bernstein conducting a master class, March 13, 1979

THE ATMOSPHERE was so wonderful: to walk past an open door on the third floor and hear music that was so rich and full that you had to stop and realize that Leonard Bernstein was teaching a conducting class, and realize that this was available to your students walking through this building, all these wonderful things. I envied my own students. I thought—"Oh! If I could have had this. If only I could have had this." **MARIAN SELDES**

DRAMA

PART OF THE mandate of the creation of
Lincoln Center was that there would be an
institutional training program as part of it.
They asked Juilliard to join, and Juilliard then
had to include a drama program, which had
not been part of Juilliard up until that time.
John Houseman and Michel Saint-Denis were
asked to head that program—Michel, because
he had started a variety of schools—The Old
Vic school in England, the National Theater
School of France at Strasbourg, and the
National Theater School in Canada. He had a
huge reputation not only as a director but also
as a theater educator. John was very well
known as both a director and a producer. So
these two titans—giants—were asked to start
the program at Juilliard. **MICHAEL KAHN**

Andre Braugher, Group 17, in title role of *Othello,* directed by Michael Langham, 1988

120

Houseman Named to Head Juilliard Drama School

By Stuart W. Little

JUILLIARD has put in a bid to join the ranks of major drama schools with the appointment of John Houseman to head a new drama division when the school moves into Lincoln Center.

Houseman is one of the most experienced directors in the country with a history of stage work going back to Mercury Theater days with Orson Welles. His appointment underlines Juilliard's designation as the over-all educational arm of Lincoln Center.

As a director, Houseman is equally familiar with films, radio and television and has also taught before at Vassar, Barnard and UCLA. He has not worked in the theater in the East since he resigned as artistic director of the American Shakespeare Festival in Stratford, Conn., in 1959.

Appointment of Houseman was announced yesterday by Peter Mennin president of the Juilliard School of Music, to become effective when the

THEATER NEWS

John Houseman, who has been named head of Drama Division of Juilliard.

Opposite: Michel Saint-Denis with John Houseman, August 1968. Houseman was director of the Juilliard Drama Division from 1968 until 1976. Saint-Denis, a brilliant theater educator who was Houseman's full partner in the development of the division, died only a few years after the division began and did not have the opportunity to see the program flourish. While Houseman continued in his role as director of the Drama Division, he also became sought after late in life as a film and television actor. A memorable accomplishment was his Academy Award—winning role as Professor Kingsfield in the film, set at Harvard Law School, *The Paper Chase*. When he stepped down from his position at Juilliard, he was succeeded by Alan Schneider, an eminent stage director whose interpretations of the plays of Samuel Beckett and Edward Albee, among others, invigorated American theater. Schneider was only at Juilliard for a short time, from 1976 to 1979. Michael Langham, the British stage director who had been director of the Stratford Festival of Canada (and later led the Guthrie Theater in Minneapolis and the Dallas Theater Center), was head of drama at Juilliard until 1992, when Michael Kahn became director of the Drama Division.

Above: *The New York Herald Tribune* announces John Houseman's selection as director of the Drama Division.

AS WE PROCEED with our preparation under the questioning eyes of Frank Damrosch, James Loeb, Felix Salmond, Ludwig van Beethoven, and Johann Sebastian Bach, you have, whether you like it or not, assumed responsibility for us—just as we have assumed the obligation and accepted the challenge of meeting, in the field of drama, the high standards set by you of the Juilliard School of Music over the years. **JOHN HOUSEMAN**

JOHN HOUSEMAN'S history was a quite extraordinary one. He had been a director, a producer...but the most important thing about John is that he was the most extraordinary "smeller out" of talent. That is what he had done from the day he met Orson Welles, all the way through his career at MGM, all the way through the Mercury Theater, all the way through the Center Theater Group that he started in L.A. He could just spot and adore talent. Plus the fact that he was a wonderful figurehead. That's why his friend James Bridges gave him the role in *The Paper Chase* where he was playing a slightly more exaggerated version of his own autocratic self! **MICHAEL KAHN**

WE HAD the sense that we were clicking into American theater history, and that's something that's always been interesting to me. I love working with people of previous generations. Anyone my age knows people who knew Stanislavski— that's how short the history of modern theater is. So that was incredible, to know people who knew Stanislavski, and to see, every day, a man who had produced plays with Orson Welles. It was invigorating and it was inspiring, and it made you want to do better work. **GREGORY MOSHER**

John Houseman and Orson Welles in the rear of the Maxine Elliot Theater on West 39th Street in New York City during a rehearsal for the WPA Theatre Project production *Horse Eats Hat,* 1936

Above: Wykeham Rise girls' school, Washington, Connecticut, Drama Division Retreat, August 1968. Just before the division's first year at Juilliard, John Houseman and Michel Saint-Denis invited the newly established Drama Division faculty and a handful students from the National Theatre School of Canada (who served as "guinea pigs" for demonstrations and training sessions), to attend the retreat. Meetings, sample classes, and discussions, both formal and informal, were held each day to help clarify and establish the techniques and curriculum for the four-year training program at Juilliard.

Left (left to right): Unidentified, Michael Kahn, John Houseman, Moni Yakim, Elizabeth Smith, and Stephen Aaron were among those who took part in the retreat. Others in attendance included Brian Bedford, Suria Saint-Denis (educator and wife of Michel Saint-Denis), Edith Skinner, Anna Sokolow, Judith Leibowitz, Hovey Burgess, René Auberjonois, William Woodman, and William Hickey, many of whom remained on The Juilliard School Drama Division faculty for many years. Michael Kahn, who has been a member of the acting faculty since the program's inception in 1968, became director of the Drama Division in 1992.

126

THE BASIC curriculum was Michel's. There was improvisation and there were movement classes and voice classes and there were masks. How the school progressed from year to year, and that the fourth year would be the performance year, was all actually written out.
MICHAEL KAHN

WE ARE TRYING to form an actor equipped with all possible means of dramatic expression, capable of meeting the demands of today's and tomorrow's ever-changing theater—an actor who is capable of participating in these changes and who is, himself, inventive enough to contribute to them. For, in the final analysis, whatever experiments may be attempted through fresh forms of writing on new stages with the latest technical devices, everything ultimately depends on the human being—the actor. **MICHEL SAINT-DENIS**

Below (left to right): Elizabeth Smith, Stephen Aaron, Barbara Goodwin, John Houseman, William Woodman, William Hickey, Lynda Goode, and Marian Fenn. Suria Saint-Denis and Michel Saint-Denis are standing, addressing the group.

MICHEL Saint-Denis's love for acting was just incredible. And I think that this inspiration had something to do with you *connecting* with him. I recall when we were at the retreat, Michel saw a mask lying on the table and he put it on and he was incredible. He was funny, he was moving. Within two minutes, he was in such total transformation that it was amazing.

Michel Saint-Denis (with Suria Saint-Denis, top, and John Houseman, above) at the Drama Division Retreat, August 1968

He was not a young man, and, of course, his wife, Suria, was screaming—she was very afraid that he might have a heart attack; he was not a well man at the time. But, he was just so magnificent and you saw so much love for what he did, that it was contagious. I think it had a lot to do with that, not less than the specifics of the techniques that he wanted us to do. **MONI YAKIM**

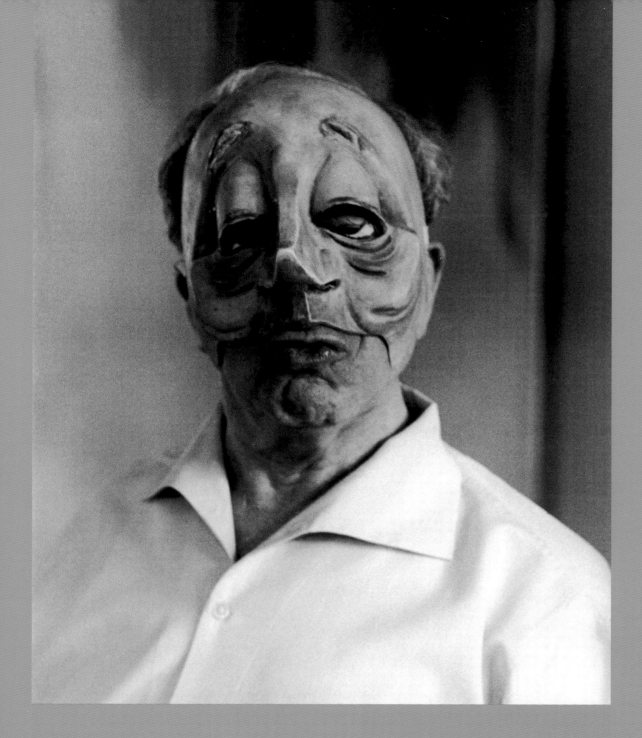

THE ATMOSPHERE, the feeling, was all of adventure. It was the beginning of a school. I think there were almost as many members of the faculty as there were students. You got to know everybody so well and all the faculty meetings were thrilling because we were students too, we were learning how to be a faculty together and I think we succeeded. **MARIAN SELDES**

WHAT JOHN Houseman wanted
was to take that kind of power
and strength that he knows
exists here [in America] and give
it some chops. Give you the ability
to do anything—to be able to pull
off Shakespeare, but do it like
Brando. To be able to give it *a feel*
and a power that we've got.
ROBIN WILLIAMS

Above: Val Kilmer and Linda
Kozlowski, Group 10, in a 1981 production of *Electra and Orestes* at
Juilliard. In the fourth year of the
drama program for each group,
the students perform a number of
plays in repertory, staged in the
Juilliard Drama Theater and open
to the public.

Left: Robin Williams, Group 6, in
a workshop production of *A
Midsummer Night's Dream*, 1974.
Workshop productions are not
open to the general public.

I THINK one of the overriding tenets of the philosophy of Saint-Denis, Houseman, and Juilliard in general, is that great actors are made from playing the great roles. The same in the music school—if you practice Bach and Rachmaninoff and Beethoven and the big hard challenging pieces, whatever your instrument, whatever your discipline, those great masterworks are what challenge you and what make you good. If you do mediocre material, if you master mediocrity —okay, so what? **KEVIN KLINE**

Above: Rehearsing *The Three Sisters*, by Anton Chekhov. Standing are three members of Group 1: Mary-Joan Negro (left), Mary Lou Rosato (right), and Patti LuPone (seated).

Left: Kelly McGillis, Group 12, in a rehearsal project, *The Three Sisters*, 1981

Juilliard Company—A School for Stars

By MEL GUSSOW

Anyone worried about the future of the American theater should see the new Juilliard Acting Company in action. This company of fourth-year students in the Drama Division at the Juilliard School is presenting (through tomorrow evening) a season of true repertory—and doing it splendidly.

Over a period of six days I saw Gorky's naturalistic drama, "The Lower Depths," Sheridan's Restoration comedy, "The School for Scandal," Middleton's 17th-century tragedy, "Women Beware Women," and — a complete change of style—a contemporary double bill of Israel Horovitz's "The Indian Wants the Bronx" and Jean-Claude van Itallie's "Interview."

This is a repertory that would challenge any company—and it does challenge Juilliard. The productions are not of uniform excellence, but each reveals, in performance, a first-rate ensemble of actors.

•

"The Lower Depths," as staged somberly by Boris Tumarin, is full of atmospheric detail and richly textured character acting. Gerald Freedman's "School for Scandal" is elegant and impudent. The most completely enjoyable production is of the least performed play, "Women Beware Women," directed by Michael Kahn. If played heavily, the intricate romantic intrigues in this play about man's manipulation of women might seem melodramatic. Played lightly they are funny. When tragedy strikes and litters the stage with corpses, the play becomes black comedy.

Least effective is Gene Lesser's staging of "The Indian Wants the Bronx," which lacks the force of the original Off Broadway production. On the other hand "Interview" is charmingly presented. Although apparently better trained for classics, the company can also play modern works.

The pleasure of spending four evenings with this company is that its members,

Mary Lou Rosato, left, and Leah Chandler in "Women Beware Women"

Henry Senber

The Cast

THE LOWER DEPTHS by Maxim Gorky; adapted by Alex Szogyl; directed by Boris Tumarin; musical direction by Gerald Shaw.
THE SCHOOL FOR SCANDAL by Richard Brinsley Sheridan; directed by Gerald Freedman; music by Robert Waldman.
WOMEN BEWARE WOMEN By Thomas Middleton; directed by Michael Kahn; music supervised by Martin Verdrager; choreography by William Burdick.
INTERVIEW by Jean-Claude Van Itallie and THE INDIAN WANTS THE BRONX by Israel Horovitz; directed by Gene Lesser.
Settings by Douglas W. Schmidt; costumes supervised by John David Ridge; lighting by Joe Pacitti. Presented by the Juilliard School, Peter Mennin, president, the Juilliard Acting Company, under the direction of John Houseman. At the Drama Workshop, 144 West 66th Street.
WITH: Leah Chandler, Benjamin Hendrickson, Cynthia Herman, Cindia Huppeler, Kevin Kline, Patti LuPone, Dakin Matthews, Anne McNaughton, James Moody, Mary Joan Negro, Mary Lou Rosato, Jared Sakren, David Schramm, Gerald Shaw, Norman Snow, David Ogden Stiers and Sam Tsoutsouvas.

as they change characters, clothes, faces and styles, grow individually and collectively before one's eyes.

•

In "The Lower Depths" Leah Chandler is a drab, dying wife. What a surprise to see her emerge, radiantly, as the romantic lead in "Women Beware Women." Mary Lou Rosato, as a peddler in "The Lower Depths" seemed noisy and abrasive. But in larger roles, as a sexually aggressive widow in "Women," and as the malicious Lady Sneerwell in "Scandal," she turns out to be sizable comic talent—perhaps too large to be contained in small parts. On the other hand, Mary Joan Negro, although outstanding in her two leading roles, is also lovely to watch as a mere scene-shifting maid.

The actors that reveal the greatest dimension—at least at this early point in Juilliard's theatrical history—are Sam Tsoutsouvas and David Ogden Stiers. Mr. Tsoutsouvas is a bitter intellectual in "Depths," a passionate uncle in "Women," and both an evil servant and a boisterous reveler in "Scandal." In "Depths" Mr. Stiers is seedy and pathetic, in "Women" polished and haughty, and in "Scandal," he is that designing cad, Joseph Surface—a fully realized, soundly comic performance.

The performers' weakness, not surprisingly, is playing old age, for which they sometimes overcompensate with pursed lips and furrowed brows. But on the other hand they have a vibrancy that enhances their playing of youth. To mention a few of many other good performances — Kevin Kline is a dashing Charles Surface, Patti LuPone a tantalizing Lady Teazle, Norman Snow a soulful poet, David Schramm a befuddled young cuckold.

The theater itself, Juilliard's Drama Workshop, is, with the possible exception of the Forum, the nicest small theater in New York. Designed by Heige Westermann (in consultation with Michel Saint-Denis) it is an intimate amphitheater with 277 seats steeply banked around a pit, on which floats a stage. Both stage and pit are used for playing. In the hands of set designer Douglas W. Schmidt, the stage is eminently convertible. Theater, scenery, costumes—the students have been given the best possible setting in which to demonstrate their talents. And they reciprocate.

The group will tour, play another season at Juilliard in May—and then graduate, to be replaced next year by another class of fourth-year students.

Instead of distributing these actors on the theatrical marketplace, why can't we keep them here, intact, as a permanently expanding company, performing great plays in repertory in this theater? Isn't there room for two theatrical companies at Lincoln Center?

The New York Times, December 16, 1971. When the first class of the Juilliard Drama Division, Group 1, reached its fourth and final year of training, John Houseman and the drama faculty were instrumental in developing that group of young actors into a professional theater repertory company. That ensemble came to be known as The Acting Company, and it continues today. The company embodies the original vision of John Houseman and Michel Saint-Denis, who wanted young actors to have the discipline and training to perform a wide range of dramatic work in regional theaters across America. Over the decades, impressive young actors have cut their teeth as members of the company, performing classic and modern works for the theater.

WE WERE the first class, and I think that the teachers and John and Michel Saint-Denis were all on the line with the prestigious music school. They had to prove they could develop American classical actors. So nobody was taking any chances! Everybody was going to make sure that we learned, regardless of how we learned…and it was costly emotionally to many of us. **PATTI LUPONE**

John Houseman and members of Group 1, in the spring of 1972, reading rave reviews of The Acting Company's first season.

THE FIRST graduating class of the newly founded Drama Division of The Juilliard School gave a season in New York that was so well received, and the kids were so impressive, that we were faced with the choice of letting them go into the world and, presumably, do well in the world, or trying to keep this very rare thing—a theatrical ensemble—together. And this was settled for us because a number of offers were received from all over the country for engagements of the company. And so, suddenly overnight, we found ourselves running a theatrical company called The Acting Company. **JOHN HOUSEMAN**

THE FIRST time I got to the school—Michael Kahn was there. And just the way he dressed, I mean he's Mick Jagger [laughs]! He was the head of the drama department. He was a very, very extreme, eccentric sort of character. **NORMAN SNOW**

MICHAEL Kahn was like Mick Jagger to me, too, whatever that means [laughs]. I just thought he was an oracle. He's still an oracle. He's still with me, you know? **JANE ADAMS**

Left: Michael Kahn rehearsing *Women Beware Women* with students from Group 1, 1971. Mary Lou Rosato recalls: "Michael taught me how to act. It wasn't easy. I remember one night, I was doing *Women Beware Women*, and I was at a crisis stage. It was either, she learns how to act or she doesn't. And I thank Michael with all my heart for eternity that he had the patience to lead me through that door. And, he stayed with me until I understood moment to moment acting. And I remember thinking, 'Oh! Oh my gosh, this is how you ride the bicycle.' And I just pedaled away"

Right: Playwrighting is now a component of the Drama Division. Left to right: Faculty members Marsha Norman and John Guare and student Brooke Berman, 1999. The Lila Acheson Wallace American Playwrights Program, under the direction of Christopher Durang and Marsha Norman, offers one-year, tuition-free, graduate level fellowships to four writers. In addition to seminars and workshops with the program directors, playwright fellows are invited to participate with acting students, directing fellows, and drama faculty in poetry classes, theater history and literature lectures, and a variety of special events. Selected playwrights may be invited to continue their studies through a second academic year to earn an Artist Diploma in Playwriting.

FOR MY AUDITON I did two monologues—one was Iago, which was a kind of compilation I had done at drama festivals in high school and had done quite well with…. So, I had a certain degree of confidence about it. What I mean by compilation is, it wasn't a strict monologue from a particular act in the play, it was a kind of piecemeal of Iago's speeches, sort of woven together to tell his story. Apparently this was looked down upon by Mr. Langham because…at the end of the audition —which you're terrified of doing, anyway—he put his glasses down on the corner of his nose, where they often rest, and sort of looked down at me and said, "I'm sorry, did you write that?" And I said, "N–no–no uh Shakespeare. It's, it's Iago." He said, "Oh I didn't recognize it." And I thought I was done. I thought I was just baked. I thought I was finished.
KEVIN SPACEY

GETTING IN THE DOOR

Christine Baranksi and Franklyn Seales,
Group 3, in a performance of John Ford's
'Tis Pity She's A Whore, directed by
Michael Kahn, 1974

I REMEMBER the moment—opening up the *Buffalo Evening News* and reading about Juilliard starting a Drama Division, and reading about John Houseman and how 1968 was to be the first year of the Drama Division, and it would be classical training. It was heart-stoppingly exciting to me. I cut the article out and pasted it on my wall, and I sent away for their brochure, which was black and opened up, and folded out—there were three or four sections about the first year of training and the second year and what you do in the third year and the fourth year. It was like this was the ultimate school. This would be like going to a great acting school in England. And it was in New York! So to me, there was no place I wanted to go more than Juilliard.

It was my dream to go to that school and I didn't get in. I was told on the phone that I was wait-listed and the problem was that I had a sibilant "S." My teeth now are not my real teeth. I had a rather large space between my teeth. And they felt that a sibilant "S" was the hardest sound to correct—it kinda whistled. They said, "If you're willing to cap your teeth to reduce the whistle and have speech therapy for the summer, we may re-audition you." So, I would say I got into that school by the skin of my teeth!

I went through speech therapy. I went back to Juilliard and into John Houseman's office, where Elizabeth Smith, the speech teacher, handed me a long paragraph of nothing but "S" words. I sat there, doing this piece with Liz's back to me, and after I finished this—trying desperately not to whistle or hiss or lisp—John said, "Elizabeth?" And, she didn't turn around. There was this long pause and then she nodded her head. And John said, "Oh, you've been accepted to Juilliard."

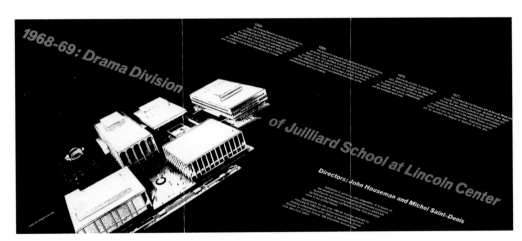

The first brochure inviting applicants to the newly created Drama Division of The Juilliard School, 1968–69

My mother was waiting for me down in Philharmonic Hall in the lobby. I told her I'd gotten in, and we went to the Algonquin Hotel and had Manhattans. That was a celebration. It was just one of the great moments of my life, getting into that school.

I was this Polish girl from Cheektowaga who had an acting dream. To me, it was just *the top.* You go to Juilliard and you walk through Lincoln Center—there is the Metropolitan Opera, and there is the New York City Ballet and there is the Philharmonic Hall and then there is Juilliard. I always had the feeling I was a part of something that had to do with *art*—with high art, the performing arts on a grand scale—and that it was a very important place to be.

CHRISTINE BARANSKI

The Juilliard Theater Center

Eriq La Salle, Group 13, with Harold Stone (standing), 1981. Stone became a member of the faculty in 1974 and was administrative director of the Drama Division from 1981 to 2001.

THE TRAGEDY a lot of times with inner-city kids such as myself is, we weren't permitted a lot of times to dream beyond our immediate environment. So, I didn't know what Juilliard was. Then I started doing research and it was a little intimidating, because I started realizing what Juilliard was and how prestigious it was. I remember the first brochure I got from the theater department —it was a picture of Keith David on the cover playing *Othello* and—phew!—It blew me away.
ERIQ LA SALLE

THE audition process… terrifying. Really. You just want to vomit the whole time you're going through it. LAURA LINNEY

Actress Laura Linney, Group 19, 1988

I WAS A little girl from Miami, Florida, wearing polyester dresses with Twiggy eyelashes. I came up to New York practically on a lark, because someone said, "They're starting a new drama department at this Juilliard school." I auditioned up at the old school. None of us knew who John Houseman and Michel Saint-Denis and Michael Kahn were, at that time. I thought I was fearless. I had nothing to gauge what I should be afraid of. I auditioned in front of these great men of the theater who had seen and directed Katharine Hepburn and worked with Laurence Olivier. I had planned to do Jocasta from *Oedipus*. I thought that'd be a nice serious piece for this group. That morning, I changed my mind and decided to do Lady Macbeth. I basically threw caution to the winds and did it. They said later it was the wildest Lady Macbeth they'd ever seen. I imagine my entire audition was pretty wild. I've always thrown myself totally into something and people have to pry me away from it. They gave us an improv—I had to pretend I was dealing with some mud. They said, "Just do what comes naturally." I remember throwing myself onto the ground and rolling in the "mud" and just rubbing it all over myself. It was an old stage and I got splinters all over myself. But I wasn't thinking of the consequences at the time. **MARY LOU ROSATO**

IT WAS QUITE clear that John Houseman and I shared a genuine interest in the person who came in who was the most unusual, the most creative, the most idiosyncratic. We gave them exercises … there's a pile of mud in front of you—what would you do? I remember Mary Lou Rosato got up and jumped in it and scraped herself along the floor and started rolling around in it like some sort of hippopotamus from *Fantasia*—We took her immediately! We thought anybody who has the guts to do that, anybody who has the freedom to do that, certainly would be an interesting student to work with. **MICHAEL KAHN**

PIANO AUDITIONS are terrible things. Nerve-racking! They're fifteen, twenty minutes long, and you've prepared at least two hours worth of repertoire, whether it's a Beethoven Sonata or a Bach Partita or a Chopin Ballade—and you have to prove your stuff within a very short period of time. I always wondered, how do they really know how good you are in fifteen minutes? How do they know that? **JULIE CHOI**

YOU LOOK AT the total entity of the student. You look at the program they picked, at their demeanor, at their sound quality. You just listen, and you get an idea of whether someone has the potential of becoming a real musician or not. After a while, you get to the point where you can tell after thirty seconds whether this is interesting or not. **VEDA KAPLINSKY**

Above: Pianist Melody Brown auditions for Julliard faculty members, 2000.

Opposite, above: Drama Division faculty members (left to right) Michael Kahn, Ralph Zito, Kate Wilson, and Harold Stone reacting to the audition of Chris Mowod (far right), 2000. Mowod went on to become a member of Juilliard's drama Group 33.

Opposite, below: Waiting in the hallway, drama auditions, 2000

I AUDITIONED with three other girls. I went to the building up on Claremont Avenue, and this very important faculty was sitting at tables at the end of the stage. I was terrified. We first had to stand in profile to the faculty so they could see if we had curvature of the spine—like you were at a horse sale—just to look at anatomy. It was like posing for a mug shot for the police. **MARTHA CLARKE**

I REMEMBER standing on the stage ... just standing up there. I did a horrible, really horrible, "Look here upon this picture," and a *Hamlet* speech that I sort of just screamed through. **BRADLEY WHITFORD**

I'LL NEVER forget my Juilliard audition. It was probably the singlemost humbling experience I've ever had. I was in the hallway with all the other fifteen or twenty oboe players from all over the world, and I'd walked in there thinking I was, you know, hot, right? And these people started to warm up, and I listened to them and I thought, "My God, this is horrible." They were—each one of them—*phenomenal*. It just *psyched me out*. I mean, if there was ever a psych-out in my life, that was it. **MARK SNOW**

141

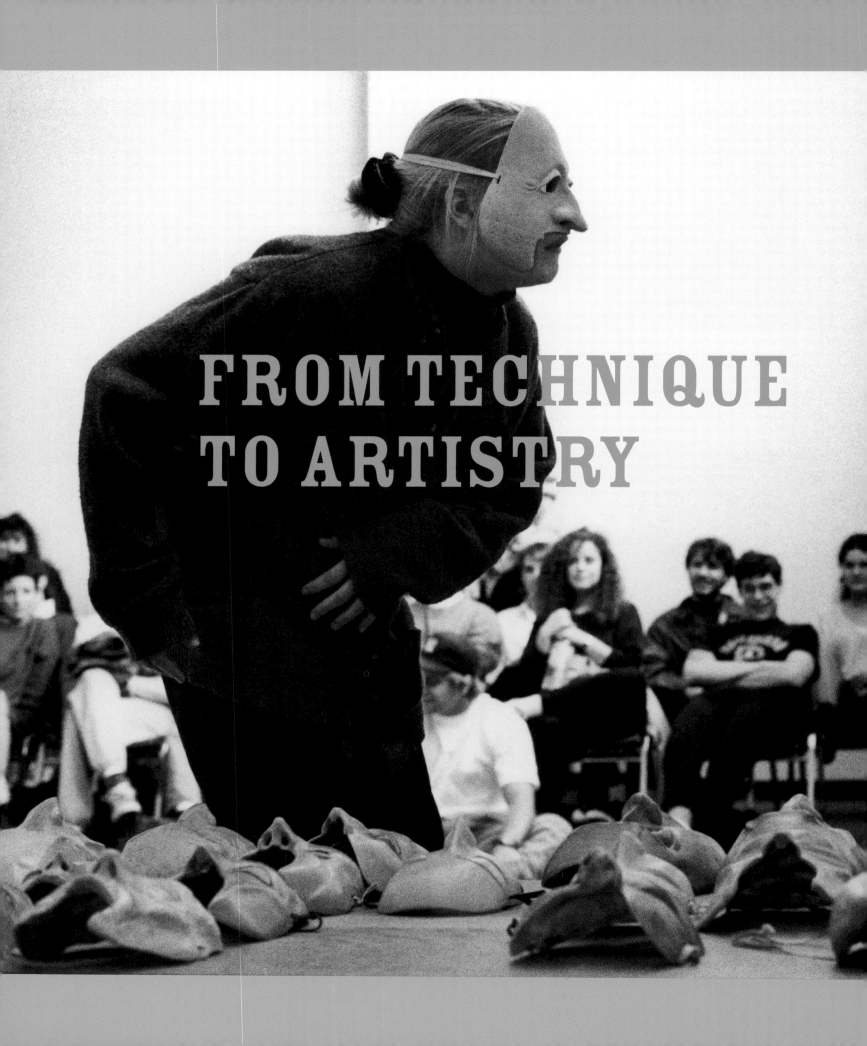

THERE IS a professional aspect to music—the craft—that is very important for any young artist to learn. As many wonderful poetic ideas as you have, there's no way you're going to be able to communicate them to another person unless you are a master of your craft. Your instrument, your voice, your body, whatever you use to express those ideas—whether you're improvising or saying something that somebody wrote down a hundred years ago—you still need to be able to go beyond the limits of your medium so art will be alive. Then, Mozart is alive in the room. When you're playing a piece of Mozart and you bring his music alive, *there he is*. He's with you, he's with all of us. That is important and ageless, something that anyone who wants to do something well must learn.

PAULA ROBISON

Mask class with Pierre Lefevre

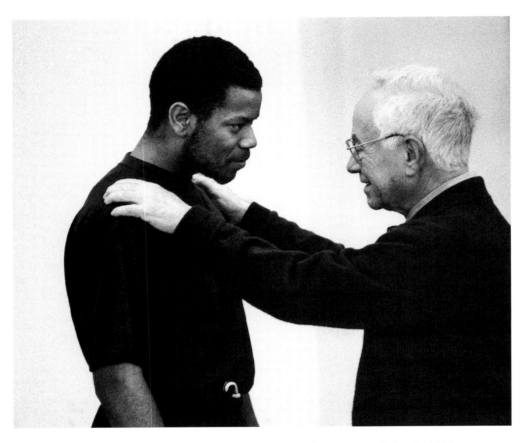

First-year acting teacher John Stix with Group 27 student Damian D. Lewis, 1994

I THINK the Juilliard Drama Division is a place where you're literally taken apart and then put back together. Your first couple of years, you're kind of deconstructed and it can be quite harrowing. But you're looking and analyzing and listening very intently because, let's face it, your body is the instrument. This is your piano, your violin, your cello. These are the strings or the keys that you have. They were picking us apart and putting us back together—which is not to say that by your fourth year, you are together. But you have the tools with which to be aware of … yourself in all different areas, so you can make use of yourself as an instrument that can be played with great subtlety and tenacity. **CHRISTINE BARANSKI**

THE [DRAMA] program is designed to take a student through four years of study. John Stix takes acting students and hands them to Eve Shapiro. Eve Shapiro takes them and hands them to Michael Kahn. Michael Kahn sort of launches you into your fourth year. And there's this layering process that happens, not only with acting, but with voice and physical movement and with the specialized classes as well—like mask and comedy classes. It's this amazing process that you don't really appreciate until you're out. **LAURA LINNEY**

YOU HAVE the sensation of the Zen getting sucked out of you. Instead of saying, "Oh, I'm going to turn the light switch on," in the first year you feel like, "Well, I'm going to lift my shoulder a little bit and then when it gets to this height I'm going to extend my elbow and then I'm just going to put my finger out and lift up to get the switch." Instead of just doing it, you break everything down. They're also sort of erasing you, shaking your Etch-a-Sketch, so you can start over. **BRADLEY WHITFORD**

YOU HAVE to take the student through a process of getting rid of an accumulation of bad habits that they've picked up very often without any knowledge that they've picked them up. That may seem like "stripping [them] bare." I don't think that's the best description of it, though, because it's, for the most part, getting rid of stuff that's not useful in the long run. Sometimes, if that's all you've got besides talent, it seems like you're left with nothing. **MICHAEL KAHN**

Left: Second-year acting teacher Eve Shapiro in class, 1983. Standing is drama student Michael Wincott, Group 15, 1983.

Below: Drama Division director Michael Kahn with members of Group 29 in a third-year acting class. A unique aspect of the program is that, when a student enters the program, he or she is part of an ensemble with all other students accepted that year and performs only with that group during the entire four-year program. Accepted into the division by audition, each student's progress is observed and assessed by the faculty, who cast plays over all four years without further auditions. The faculty members try to share the lead roles among as many students as possible and stretch the students' capabilities while they are still in a "safe" environment at school. Students still rush to the bulletin board to see who has the leading roles, and competition is understandably fierce.

AT JUILLIARD, the faculty was looking for actors who could effortlessly go from Sam Shepard one night to Tennessee Williams, to Shakespeare, to the Greeks, to *She Stoops to Conquer*. One of the things you need there is skill, versatility, and believability in speech. And it's not accidental that Houseman hired Edith Skinner as the first faculty member. Speech was a cornerstone of the training. I don't know how much the training has changed, but for my twelve years there, it was very, very important. It wasn't just Edith. When I was there, we had four faculty members in voice and speech for a lot of that time—Edith, Elizabeth Smith, Robert Williams, and myself. So it was a team effort, and we all taught slightly differently. **TIM MONICH**

EDITH SKINNER was one of the last truly eccentric people.... She was like that character that Maggie Smith played—Miss Jean Brodie. You know, "My girls are the 'créme de la créme.'"... She taught you to appreciate a short vowel and a true diphthong and how to recoil from an off-glide, an off-glide being that little eh at the end of a word—which you don't want to do unless you're an evangelical preacher who does off-glides all the time. But it doesn't work if you're doing Chekhov or Shakespeare.... She would beat any regionalism out of your speech. We would say, "But Edith, I went home at Christmas break and my friends said that I sounded phony," and she would say, "Change your friends!" **KEVIN KLINE**

Opposite, above: Tim Monich

Opposite, below: Edith Skinner (seated, center) surrounded by colleagues at the drama retreat at the Wykeham Rise School, August 1968. Left to right: John Houseman, Margaret Freed, Hovey Burgess, Edith Skinner, Brian Bedford, Judith Leibowitz, and Michael Kahn

Above: Robert Neff Williams with students

ROBERT WILLIAMS had probably the most lasting impression upon me. I always saw him as a Restoration kind of guy—built like a pipe cleaner. Oscar Wilde, in a moment. He taught us how to technically deliver a line that, if you're not feeling inspired on the fourth performance of the play, you must give and get the laugh every time, just by the way you drop it. He never judged us as students. He just loved us…by giving us the information for free. **DIANE VENORA**

WE TRY to make student actors aware of the power and the beauty and the excitement of language, and to love words. Then we must teach a technique for making those words alive. That requires clear, unaffected diction, a rich, resonant voice, variety of pace and melody, and a feeling for rhythm. Finally, we should give student actors some sense of how wonderfully exciting it is to be able to present the great classics of dramatic literature to an audience. **ROBERT NEFF WILLIAMS**

Opposite, above: Elizabeth Smith in second-year speech class, 1996-97

Opposite, below: Ralph Zito with students, 1995. A drama student in Group 14, he now teaches voice and speech at Juilliard.

Above: Drama students demonstrate for faculty, 1983

BASICALLY, we are bounded by gravity. We have this constant pull that drags us down. Our struggle is like a tree whose branches want to reach up to the sky but the roots keep pulling downward. This is the need we have as artists—to soar. In a sense that's what I do. I physicalize that need to soar, to rise, to be uplifted. And yet, the drama of it is that we are constantly pulled down. Philosophically, this is one of the aspects on which we work—to find the drama in the physicality itself.

Movement is acting through physical expression, because there is not just "movement," per se. When you move, it has to be justified, it has to be meaningful. It's not movement for its own sake. The actors are justified in whatever action they take, in whatever intention they have, and whatever situation they are in. They have to motivate it, they have to base it on their reality within the situation. That's what movement does. It's either "acting through movement," or "physical acting." **MONI YAKIM**

149

I REMEMBER doing *A Midsummer Night's Dream.* I had this shtick that I worked out with a little stocking cap that was very tight. But if I moved my eyeballs, the thing went whooop! I remember it was the very first piece of physical business, and I saw Houseman laugh. I went, "Buddha laughed! I have done well! I am now a Master!" That was kind of the beginning of going, "Hmmm, this works. This is interesting."
ROBIN WILLIAMS

Left: Robin Williams, Group 6, in rehearsal for
A Midsummer Night's Dream, 1974

Opposite, above: Second-year combat class with Felix Ivanov (right foreground) 1998–99

Opposite, below: Val Kilmer in Ellen Lauren's Suzuki class

ANOTHER great kind of physicalization [is] putting you in touch with your physicality and with the physical world. I mean, what does it mean to walk against the wind? That's an important question for any actor to ask himself. You get on a movie set and they say, "It's really a windy day but if we put the wind machine up *full*, we're going to get a bad sound-track. So, can you walk as if it's windier?" I remember in the movie, *The Ice Storm*, we shot it in May, and I had to slip on ice (which was really basically hair gel, some slime they'd put on the ground that was highly reflective and looked like ice). My training came in handy because I knew how to slip and slide on ice that wasn't really there. **KEVIN KLINE**

I WANTED to go to Juilliard because it's very hard to do Shakespeare. I knew that it's hard to speak and it's hard to move (and move consistently) and it's *really* hard to do those things if you're from the San Fernando Valley in California. **VAL KILMER**

I REMEMBER Pierre Lefevre's mask class, which was one of my favorite classes. He had a series of masks, maybe fifteen or twenty of them, different sizes, different shapes, different meanings—an old man, young man, neutral, woman—and you could put these masks on and they would cover everything but your mouth. And when you'd stand in front of a mirror, you'd see a different face than the one you know. You'd suddenly allow yourself to start taking on what you were thinking in your imagination. What body would go with that face? It begins to train you to let go of yourself.

KEVIN SPACEY

Above: Kevin Spacey, drama Group 17. The studies with masks encourage actors to transform and transcend their physical identity and habits of speech and reach into themselves to find different characters and economic ways of moving and speaking. In their first year, students use masks that fully cover the face, known as *basic masks*, and they do not speak. Representing the "four ages of man," these masks allow the students to search for their inner child as well as step into the skin of an old person. In the second year, students advance to *character masks*, half-masks (mouth uncovered) that allow speech. Mask work was central to the curriculum and training developed by Michel Saint-Denis, who brought his colleague Pierre Lefevre to Juilliard. Lefevre was known for his outstanding work with actors using mask technique in training. The training is designed to free students from inhibitions and encourage transformation. Many students remember this as one of their most beloved classes at Juilliard.

Above: Diane Venora, Group 6, working with Pierre Lefevre to develop her character for a production of *Royal Gambit*

Right: Elizabeth McGovern, Group 12, with Pierre Lefevre

IT WAS PIERRE'S spirit that most attracted me to him. He had the light—the luminescence—of a person who had lived a great deal. I had heard the stories that he was the voice of the Free French during the war ... and I had such respect for him ... The information he imparted to us seemed ... profound. I thought there was a silliness about us, all standing around in leotards and taking ourselves extremely seriously, but Pierre seemed to have that kind of ignition that made you want to listen. He would start up your engine. He remains one of the great highlights of my experience there. **KELSEY GRAMMER**

THE MASKS were great.... They were great character masks. Years later, when I did prosthetics with *Mrs. Doubtfire*, all that stuff came to mind—working with a mask to find the body and all the movements. The other side was to work from within, using all the other acting techniques to build exterior and interior. And it all worked. It was weird. All this stuff that was drilled into you made sense.... That's the ideal for me—to totally transform. I guess that was the first taste of it.... It was a freedom I loved. Because you're standing behind [the mask], at work *in* it. It's not your self, directly. There's a kind of a buffer. And that was the beginning—with him. **ROBIN WILLIAMS**

...YOU PUT on a mask and it's something that is completely light and quick and mercurial. And you begin to behave in your body, in your voice, and in your mentality, like this other creature.... That liberates people to dare to improvise text.... One of the great things I've learned to do with the masks is to make the actor conscious that everything he does must be significant for the audience. Everything he uses, in terms of his imagination or his thoughts, must find an expression. Like being a dancer. Your next impulse is going to mean something. **PIERRE LEFEVRE**

Above: The cast of Juilliard's 1971 production of Richard Brinsley Sheridan's *School for Scandal* included Kevin Kline, Patti LuPone, and David Ogden Stiers, all members of the Drama Division's first graduating class.

Opposite: Drama student Thomas Gibson, Group 14, with Judith Leibowitz. The Alexander Technique is utilized throughout the school in all disciplines. Today, the Alexander Technique faculty at Juilliard includes Jaye Dougherty, Carolyn Serota, Jane Kosminsky, and Lauren Schiff, several of whom studied with Judith Leibowitz before joining the faculty.

IT'S A DANGEROUS profession, physically. Nobody thought about that in my day. Nobody talked about, "Be careful how you stand." There was no Alexander Technique that we were aware of—everyone I know who is my age has a lot of aches and pains and problems from playing their instruments. It's a very awkward thing to do, to stand or sit in a position every day for many hours. It's going to eventually catch up with you. There was no awareness in the sixties that you had to be careful how you played.... It was not maybe even until the seventies, that for the first time there was awareness that it was dangerous to your health to be a musician. Now, I'm very aware of arts medicine and I think it's a great leap forward and a tremendous aid for musicians.
EUGENIA ZUKERMAN

ONE OF THE great classes is in the Alexander Technique. I was lucky to be taught by Judy Leibowitz. The process of the Alexander Technique is about examining physical habits, and [for example] not necessarily be bound by the way you normally get out of a chair. There is a more efficient way for your body to get out of a chair. There is a way to let your body work as it was designed to...so we're not walking around...holding all this tension. It's all about providing you with the best kind of active relaxation, which can allow you to do work as an actor.... It started to help you understand objectively what kind of choices you can physically make about characters you were playing...that whole way of thinking about process can be applied to any part of your life. The idea that you avoid being hemmed in by habits that are not necessarily chosen with any direction in mind, but which might be arbitrarily chosen, is [something] to consider. **THOMAS GIBSON**

155

IT WASN'T until I really got to Juilliard that piano became not just a hobby, or even a very important hobby, but it became the thing that kept me on track, that was as important as food or sleep. It became something that I was very much dependent on. I had never thought about sound to anywhere close to the degree to which my teacher was talking about it and to which I now think about it. I never thought about how specific you can get with the sound that you create on the

piano… the variety of moods and shades and colors that the instrument allows you to create if you learn how to do it and if you're specific with your intention. And that has become the most important thing that I have worked on. **ELIZABETH MORGAN**

Opposite, above: Pianist Elizabeth Morgan, who was featured in the *American Masters* documentary *Juilliard* in 2000

Opposite: Pianist György Sándor studied with Bartók and Kodaly at the Liszt Academy of Music in his native Budapest. A foremost interpreter of Bartók's works, he premiered the composer's Third Piano Concerto with the Philadelphia Orchestra under Eugene Ormandy in 1946. He has recorded all of Bartók's solo piano compositions, as well as the complete piano repertoire of Prokofiev and Kodály. A member of Juilliard's piano faculty since 1982, he is seen here coaching a student ensemble on a work by Janáček.

Above: Pianist and Juilliard faculty member Joseph Kalichstein coaching Juilliard students Frank Rosenwein, oboe, Edward Parsons, bassoon, and Lin Hong, piano, for a performance of Mozart's Quintet in E-flat Major, K. 452, for piano, oboe, clarinet, horn, and bassoon at ChamberFest 2002 in January 2002. The other members of the ensemble were Adam Simonsen, clarinet, and Louis Schwadron, horn. Kalichstein studied with Edward Steuermann and Ilona Kabos at Juilliard. He has presented solo recitals and concerto performances with orchestras around the world and is a member of the Kalichstein-Laredo-Robinson Trio.

HOW MANY hours does it take to develop a virtuoso piano technique? You think if you practice maybe four or five hours almost every day of the year, for maybe 5 years…? Or would it take six years? You could do the math. Fifteen hundred hours a year for maybe five years? Maybe we're up to about 7,000 now? Is it 7,000—10,000 hours? Is that enough to develop a virtuoso technique? Maybe somebody else takes 20,000 hours to develop that technique. Ultimately, it's a question of just that investment, because it isn't really so much about some kind of inherent ability—that's part of it, but a very small part of it. I'm convinced that almost anybody could learn how to play the piano. What it takes is that kind of absolutely blind commitment to it— blind in the sense that you're not going to say, "Well, gee, it doesn't make sense to spend 10,000 hours practicing the piano!" If you believe that, then you can't do it! One thing my teacher at Juilliard said a long time ago, and I thought at the time it seemed kind of naïve but I now realize how true it is—he said the only thing necessary for achieving a virtuoso technique at the piano is the desire to achieve it. When you think anybody could do that, of course you realize that's the most difficult part. It's not the hours at the instrument, it's the will that will allow you to sit there for all those hours and do it! That's the hard part.

BRUCE BRUBAKER

I SEE PROCESS in everything. And to understand that you're always in process means that you aren't bored. Dancers have to learn to love the process of it, so that the almost ritualistic acts they perform during the day—for example their classwork and rehearsals—have to be performed with a kind of intensity of focus that pays them back somehow. **BENJAMIN HARKARVY**

I REALLY want to touch the audience, make them sit up in their chairs like—"Oh! I felt that when he did that!" And I think that's what I offered when I auditioned [for Juilliard] because I wanted them to enjoy me! **ABDUR-RAHIM JACKSON**

Juilliard dance student Abdur-Rahim Jackson rehearsing in a dance studio at Juilliard, with guest artist Matthew Rushing of the Alvin Ailey Dance Company, working on Rushing's piece *Fallen Angel*, 2000. Dancer-choreographer Rushing is a role model for Jackson and other Juillard students. After Jackson's graduation from Juilliard, he joined the Ailey Company, thrilled to dance side by side with one of his mentors.

TEACHERS AND MENTORS

THEY SAY the most exclusive club in the United States is supposed to be the United States Senate. But I think they're wrong. Because, at Juilliard, the faculty... is the most exclusive club. **WILLIAM VACCHIANO**

Opposite: Leonard Rose coaching Frederick Zlotkin with Marioara Trifan at piano, c. 1971. Zlotkin is the brother of conductor and Juilliard alumnus Leonard Slatkin.

Below: Rosina Lhévinne performing with the Juilliard String Quartet, c. 1959

MY DREAM was to study with Rosina Lhévinne, who always represented the high-water mark of piano pedagogy. I think anybody interested in the piano at that time, at least in the circles in which I traveled, thought that she was the best teacher we had in our country. Then, as now, we thought that Juilliard was the best institution for higher training in music. Mrs. Lhévinne was involved with her students at a core level, and was loving, nurturing, instructing, always bringing out the best in them. Her focus was always on the cultural and human aspects of what we were studying.... She was certainly one of the great influences in my life, and I reminisce with joy and appreciation for what my brief time with her has caused to linger within me.
JOHN WILLIAMS

Above: Piano faculty, 1962. Standing, left to right: Edward Steuermann, Adele Marcus, Lonny Epstein, Katherine Bacon, Mark Schubart (Juilliard's dean), James Friskin, Sascha Gorodnitzki, Frances Mann, Alton Jones, Josef Raieff, Irwin Freundlich, and Beveridge Webster. Seated at the piano is Rosina Lhévinne.

Below: Rosina Lhévinne and her husband, Josef, came to America together and began teaching at Juilliard in 1924. According to pianist Emanuel Ax, "Josef Lhévinne was the first great virtuoso on the level of Rachmaninoff or Hoffman or Horowitz to also be a great teacher."

IN ALL THE years I worked with Rosina Lhévinne, she used to ask me my opinion of musical questions in the pieces she was performing. And I was just a kid. I was, at first, very daunted by that. But I gradually understood it. She didn't want to be out of touch with the ideas and points of view of people in younger generations than hers. That was one of the things that kept her a vital force for such a long time. She was 76 years old when I started studying with her and she lived into her mid 90s.... She was a tiny lady with a fantastic sensitivity and will, and an extraordinary pianist! There was so much to learn from her. Even though she knew that I didn't intend to spend my life with the big piano solo pieces, she loved chamber music so much [and]

she loved song literature so much, she appreciated that I wanted to conduct and she went on teaching me anyway because she respected the whole idea of a musician having a broad education.

She had, after all, brought me to a much higher level of accomplishment at the instrument than I would have been able to get with someone who didn't understand what my whole musical personality was about. It's a very very two way street. My relationship with her was extraordinary.

I played all kinds of repertoire for her, and she made very perceptive critiques... I had a dialogue with her all the time. Just as she wanted to know my point of view, I wanted exactly the same from her. She had a whole half of her life...in Russia and in Europe in a kind of musical atmosphere that was totally different than the one I had when I was growing up in Middle America. **JAMES LEVINE**

I PRESSED my nose against the window of Juilliard—by studying with Samaroff…. She was a queen, a great lady. She was the career maker. That's why every pianist wanted to study with her. She had developed people like Rosalyn Tureck and Eugene List, and Willie Kapell [William Kapell] who was my contemporary. She had connections…. She was a great musician and a fine piano teacher. But the really special thing was her connections with conductors, managers, and wealthy people. Her master classes weren't really master classes at all. They were grand parties where the students had to dress up—boys in black tie, girls in evening dresses. We would play for this distinguished audience. There wouldn't be criticism of the performance. It was a real audition for these important people. So, it was terrifying and wonderful. But that was Samaroff—it was an atmosphere, an aura. She had a great apartment on Fifth Avenue, a limousine with a chauffeur, and butlers and maids. Champagne was served. That was Olga Samaroff…. We were introduced to real New York and international musical life and social life. She would send her students to the Metropolitan Museum or take them to the opera. I won't mention some of the famous cases, but some of them she took into her home, and she would teach them how to walk and how to dress. Yes, she really opened doors.

JOSEPH BLOCH

Above: Olga Samaroff with students Solveig Lund Madsen and William Kapell, just after *juries*, the year-end assessment of students' progress by faculty, Claremont Avenue, 1942. Pianist Samaroff gained recognition as a performer around 1905. Born Lucie Hickenlooper in Texas in 1882, she changed her name, as legend goes, because she recognized that foreign-born artists and teachers were given more attention and respect in America. She married conductor Leopold Stokowski and, the year after they divorced, in 1924, she began teaching at the newly founded Juilliard Graduate School. At the time, she was the only American-born member of the piano faculty.

Left: Adele Marcus was on the faculty at Juilliard from 1954 until 1990. As children, Marcus and her sister, Rosamund, formed a piano duo and were known as the Two Prodigies. At fifteen, Marcus auditioned for Josef Lhévinne and, soon after, became his pupil, and then, for seven years, his assistant. A renowned performer in the Romantic style, she ultimately made teaching and master classes the core of her professional life. Many of her students at Juilliard went on to illustrious performing careers.

Dorothy DeLay working with her student Nadja Salerno-Sonnenberg, 1980

IT'S DIFFICULT TO describe how Dorothy DeLay teaches. When I first went to her I was fourteen years old and had a lot of bad problems—technical bad habits that I had developed. I wasn't thinking yet. Everything was by instinct. I was very rebellious. What she had to do at that point, more than anything, was be a psychiatrist. Later, when I was older, and I started to think about the process of playing and whether I really want to do this the rest of my life, our relationship changed.

There are certain things she does, certain methods that are phenomenal and work.

THE mutual learning that's going on is incredible. I think that's what's important. I learn from my kids so much. **DOROTHY DELAY**

She teaches each student differently—emotionally and psychologically. And I think she spoke to students in the language that they hear. At fourteen years old, to hear, "Well, Sugar Plum, your vibrato is not varied enough. . . . I have other students that can do a finger vibrato, and can do a wrist vibrato, and an arm vibrato, and you just have a finger vibrato," or if she had said, "You need to do this first, followed by this, followed by that, and end with this," . . . I simply wouldn't have heard that! She knew how to talk to me, how to make it seem like it was my idea, how to make it seem like it was a really good idea if I did this, and if I *did* this, then I'd be even cooler than I am now. She was extraordinarily smart that way. **NADJA SALERNO-SONNENBERG**

MY FIRST EXPOSURE was to Miss DeLay . . . and then to Ivan Galamian, who was my teacher as well. It was a very good one-two punch combination of teachers, probably the greatest ever. Their styles were totally different. Their systems were basically the same technically, but their approaches were different. Galamian would say, basically, "Do this. Do that. If you do this, that'll happen." Just follow orders. Miss DeLay would say, "Sugarplum, what is your concept of G sharp?" meaning, it's out of tune. She would never say something is wrong or right. She would always try to make you figure it out, make you think about it, make you participate in the lesson rather than follow orders. I remember going into Studio 518 at the old Juilliard on Claremont Avenue—with Mr. Galamian. I couldn't see the room because he would smoke and the room was filled with smoke. It was like going into a total fog. I would say, "Mr. Galamian, where are you? Oh, over there!" He would sit in the corner. I remember

Ivan Galamian in his New York studio, 1977

being very, very nervous when I would play for him. He had very penetrating eyes, and he would look at you and say, "It's out of tune." Like a god, you know? So, I would go into that room and be scared to death. I would play the piece and try very hard, and he would say, "Yes, do this. No, do this. You're not doing that . . ." Then I remember leaving the room and going home to practice, and I would immediately feel just as nervous practicing by myself as when I was playing for Galamian. I couldn't figure it out. Then one day I realized that the cigarette smoke was still in my violin. As I was practicing, it was coming out into my nose, and it gave me this flavor of Galamian all over again. I said, "Oh, my God!" That's when I realized how frightened I was, but he did not play power games. Every student who came to study with him got the same thing, his best. I think that is a sign of a great teacher: that no one is special. You got one hour of everything he had to offer. **ITZHAK PERLMAN**

165

Leonard Slatkin conducting

A MONDAY in school with Morel was spent in front of two pianos, with the conductors dividing up the music of the score, and one person conducting. We would take what we learned on Monday into the orchestra situation on Thursday. In addition to observing every rehearsal that he or his colleagues did, we got very involved in all activities relating to orchestras, whether they were for the opera, for symphony concerts, or for ballet. That amounted to immersion into the world of how conducting is taught. As Morel used to tell us, "Don't imitate what I do. Watch me. And when I make mistakes, keep that in mind, and try to avoid making the mistakes." That was part of his teaching method. Another part of it was to always remind us of what our mistakes were. And he was merciless! He sent some of the students crying off the podium—he really did. The more talented you were, the less likely he was to even issue a compliment. In my fourth year, my last year, I did a performance of *American in Paris*. I thought it went well. Very rarely do I think very highly of anything I do. I ran into [Room] 304, where Morel was sitting behind his desk, chomping on that cigar—we never really saw him light it much, he just sort of chewed on it—because I knew he would have to say something good, finally, after four years. I knocked. "Yes, come in." I came in. He didn't look up from his desk. Finally, he said, "Slatkin, well, it was not bad." Well, that was the highest compliment I got in the whole four years, but it meant everything to me because somehow I'd broken through a little bit. And to this day, I think every time I come off the stage, inside me, if I believe it may have gone well, I'll always say, "It wasn't bad." **LEONARD SLATKIN**

ANY OF US who survived Juilliard under the years of the tyranny of Jean Morel talk about the *Morelisms*, because he would shout and shriek at the orchestra. I first became aware of my first husband when Morel was having a tantrum and yelling at everyone, "Saboteur! Gangster! I kill you!" And then he suddenly wheeled around and pointed at this young boy at the back of the first violin section and said, "Zukerman, out!" Whenever anything happened it was Zukerman's fault and he would throw Pinky Zukerman out of orchestra, send him down to the dean's office, and there would be a big brouhaha and then the next rehearsal Zukerman would be there again, sitting in the back. **EUGENIA ZUKERMAN**

Jean Morel

Julius Baker

JULIUS BAKER is a very interesting character. He was very demanding as a teacher. We had to bring certain [pieces] in and they had to be memorized. They had to be perfect. He was someone who taught by example, not by speaking or explaining. If you would say to him, "How do you get that beautiful low D?" He would say, "Oh it's easy. Like this." And he would play it. I think so much of music-making is imitating sound.... Hearing Julius Baker was so exquisite. There hasn't been anyone who has been able to really copy that sound. Baker gave individual lessons and also had group meetings, and those had a competitive edge to them as all of these things do. Very few teachers are able to create an atmosphere where there's no competition, but everybody wanted to play really well and please him. **EUGENIA ZUKERMAN**

JULIUS BAKER'S sound is... so beautiful, like a ripe peach in the sun. Most of us who have studied with him come away with that feeling of, "How can *I* do that? How can I play like he does?" He's a teacher who doesn't analyze things deeply—he plays. So, the sound that he would play in lessons was something that we all carried away with us and tried to emulate. It's quite like a precious jewel. **PAULA ROBISON**

ROGER SESSIONS was the teacher who I spent the most time with, and he was one of the most important people in my life. While I was working with him, I felt like I came into my own. I discovered my own voice and who I was. He was not anyone who wanted to discipline somebody to write like he did, or to adopt exactly his points of view. It's very interesting that if you look at the subsequent history of American composition, Sessions's pupils are really quite visible today. He taught perhaps four generations of people, many of whom have come to the fore. He was a gentle and philosophical quiet man who was a wonderful support as a teacher. **ELLEN TAAFFE ZWILICH**

Ellen Taaffe Zwilich with Roger Sessions, early 1970s

167

YOU RESPOND to teachers who you feel you have something in common with. As a student, you don't really know who you are and what you want, but suddenly somebody gives you a spawning ground—a place to grow in—and it feels right. **MARTHA CLARKE**

WHEN WE SIT and watch these young people dance, we're overwhelmed with the responsibility we have toward them. I come away from the first workshop of each year in the studio and I'm so moved by their openness, their vulnerability, their idealism, their talent! We knew there was talent there, but when you see these other things that you hope are there and it's all out there, your sense of responsibility to them is enormous. As human beings and as dancers, we're there at a very important formative point in their lives. **BENJAMIN HARKARVY**

Opposite, above: June Dunbar (kneeling next to male student) in a modern dance class, c. 1960s

Opposite, below: Ethel Winter instructing Emilie Plaunché in advanced modern dance class, November 1986

Above: Benjamin Harkarvy and alumnus Robert Battle observe a rehearsal for Battle's *Baseline,* which was commissioned for the fiftieth anniversary of the Dance Division and performed in February 2002. The score for Battle's work was composed by Victor L. Goines, artistic director of Juilliard's Institute for Jazz Studies.

Antony Tudor demonstrating for his students in his ballet arrangement class, early 1960s

I REMEMBER the day he walked into the studio for the first time with that back and that neck—this kind of hawklike, predatory-looking man. It was amazing. There were psychological tests for you. They were embarrassing—sexual innuendo all over the place. Talk about politically incorrect! He was an incredible force in my life, and everyone else's life.... I had always felt the teachers at Juilliard were also mentors. I think of all of the things Tudor taught me about—Martinu and Bartók, and the books he gave me to read, *Zen and the Art of Archery*. In his explorations, he finally moved to the Zendo. He created the Zen Institute in New York. He took me to the Roshi; we sat and meditated together. He took me to a yoga teacher, so I'd have some knowledge of what was going on in Hatha yoga. This was way beyond teaching you how to do a plié or tende. Tudor and Limón, as well—these were *artists*, well-rounded artists who had a broad knowledge and were always talking to you about the other art forms, what was going on, and what you should be seeing to become a better artist. **BRUCE MARKS**

TUDOR IS the only teacher I ever had I would have taken my skin off for. I remember it was like being in love! I remember every day going to school and wanting to please this man, you know? It was nearly a love affair! It was like a flirtation. Obviously, he was not interested, but there was a feeling of wanting to take in everything from him! He was elegant. He was ironic. He was twisted. He was perverse. He was a little cruel. But he had a wonderful sense of humor. He did often make students cry, but he liked me, and he never made me cry. **MARTHA CLARKE**

WITH EACH person, you have a different story and a different relationship. But with Antony Tudor it was very, very special. I took many classes with him, not only at Juilliard—I also went to his class at the Metropolitan Opera. I always took his classes... so I was always around and I learned very much. Maybe I was also lucky because he could be very nasty to certain people or be very forward and [he had a] very strange [sense of] humor, but never with me. Ours was always a very beautiful relationship. He gave me many possibilities. **PINA BAUSCH**

Left, above: Antony Tudor with Ruth Mesavages and Susan Theobald

Left, below: Antony Tudor with Susan Theobold and Francia Dolores Roxin

Right, above and below: Tudor rehearsing *A Choreographer Comments* with Pina Bausch at Juilliard, c. 1959

Below: Fellow dance students Mercedes Ellington and Pina Bausch at Juilliard, c. 1959

SOMETIMES, it was strange—these big people like Antony Tudor or José Limón, who I admired so much. When you saw them out in the corridor, they didn't speak to each other. I couldn't understand. I don't know what problem they had. But when they met, they just passed by, not looking at each other— like two kings passing by. That's very strange for somebody young to understand. These fantastic people—what happened between them? I still don't know, but it was very interesting.
PINA BAUSCH

Right: José Limón teaching at Juilliard, February 1959

Opposite, José Limón, c. 1964–65

JOSÉ LIMÓN'S association with Juilliard was enormous and Juilliard was an enormous influence on him, in that Martha Hill gave him a space in which to work. The Limón Company was actually based at Juilliard for many years. His choreography and his contribution to the image of the male dancer were extraordinary. I mean, there was nothing prissy about José. He was a very strong and magnificent presence.
MURIEL TOPAZ

VOCALLY and visually, Limón was the most outgoing of all. He was who he was twenty-four hours a day. When you met him in the hallway, he'd say, "Bruce, my son, how are you?" He'd grab your shoulder, show you his profile. Talk about larger than life! That was Limón. He was himself on the stage and in the studio and in the hallway—he was a huge, huge figure. He and his dance were so different than Graham. Graham was mythological, symbolic, and dramatic. Limón was about humanity, about our foibles. Both of them were playing their heroes. It was clear that Graham was going to do every mythological Greek woman that existed. Limón was doing these tragic, huge men—*Lament for Ignacio Sánchez Mejias*. All of his male roles were the great Napoleonic figures, the great big tragic human figures. Graham and Limón were actually complementary in a way, but very different in approach. **BRUCE MARKS**

ANNA SOKOLOW was a disciple of Martha Graham and then went off on her own. She also taught at The Actor's Studio—she taught Brando, among other people. Her class [at Juilliard] was amazing. If she saw you doing a push-up she'd say, "What the hell is that? I don't want to ever see a movement without an emotion attached to it." So, class started with us reaching on our tiptoes, reaching for the sky. She'd walk around and pull your hair if you weren't reaching with every fiber of your being. Then, she'd get us doing not modern dance, but close to that—moving, but always with emotion. She was teaching us that certain movements could almost induce an emotion, and how the emotional life and the physical life are inextricably intertwined. She was very much from the old school. I remember one day she said, "If it doesn't hurt, it ain't art."
KEVIN KLINE

ANNA. Man, what a character. She would not allow you to smile in class because she thought it was a cheap emotion that she would call *bullshit*. "This isn't about smiling." She would choreograph these dances about horrible things—you know, Auschwitz—and asking God, "Why?" She was a passionate, dark woman who worked with Martha Graham. There was a rumor she had had an affair with Eugene O'Neill. She was this legendary woman. She would come up to you and, in the middle of class without a segue, grab you and say, "Is it a crime to be poetic?" And walk away. **BRADLEY WHITFORD**

Anna Sokolow working with a student

THE FIRST time I went into Anna's class she said, "Okay everybody lie down. Now, turn over on your stomach. Reach your arms out. Reach your legs out. Now, jump [laughs]." If you can imagine, you are lying flat on your stomach, there's no way you can jump. But that epitomizes who she was—she always demanded the impossible and mostly got it.
MURIEL TOPAZ

Michael Kahn with John Rolle, drama Group 30, 1999

YOU HAVE this new set of parents, in a way, who are trying to mold you and guide you and criticize you and lean on you and make sure you're doing it right. At the same time, you are forging your identity as an actor, as an artist, as a human being. As such, it's sort of like adolescent kids with parents. There can be a dynamic tension where you respect them but you hate them, and you rebel against them but you also acceed to their demands.
KEVIN KLINE

MICHAEL Kahn said great things [like]—"Mr. Williams, what you've just done is a bit like someone urinating in brown corduroy pants. You feel wonderful. We see nothing."
ROBIN WILLIAMS

THAT LINE about pissing in brown corduroy pants —I don't remember, but I could have said it. I truly could have said it. I wish I remembered saying it because it sounds like fun.
MICHAEL KAHN

MICHAEL KAHN is the best acting teacher in the world. And that he is the head of the Drama Division now is fitting, right, and perfect! The man who was there at the beginning is now running it. What better bliss than that? He's a brilliant man. I wonder if he was born that way, if he was born with all the smarts he ever needed. If you've ever seen any of the plays he's directed, they're full of passion, imagination, and extravagance. He's such a man of *theater*. And we don't have many—we don't have many visionaries left. **MARY LOU ROSATO**

I REMEMBER one day I was walking down Seventh Avenue with another student, and he pointed across the street and said, "Do you see that woman over there, standing on the corner wearing purple?" I said, "Yes." He said, "That's one of your teachers, that's Marian Seldes." I said, "Really? Oh! I want to meet her." So, we went across the street and he said, "Marian, this is Kevin. He's going to be in your first class." And Marian, who is this beautiful being, sort of held my face in

her hands and she said, "My little bird." And she ran off down the street, not looking one way or the other at traffic, just kind of gone. She was just flitting through Manhattan. And I thought, "Who is that woman?" And my friend said, "God has his finger on her head and he just lets her go through life. He protects her." **KEVIN SPACEY**

WHEN I got to school, they had a kind of coffee brunch thing, and Marian Seldes came over and just burst through and said, "Oh, my bird!" She was the tallest woman I had ever met, and just the most beautiful woman and just so wonderful. I thought, "Oh, it's going to be okay. There are crazy people here, I'm going to be fine [laughs]." And I mean *crazy* in the best sense of the word when I'm talking about Marian. She's theatrical, you know. She's big.
JANE ADAMS

WHAT I loved about Marian was that she was so loving toward us. She was like this great mother who adores her children. When you were with Marian, you felt you could open up and be wonderful. She looked at you like you were the most wonderful thing and so you blossomed in front of Marian and were maybe a little more daring or a little more open because she's just loving. You know she's very nurturing. And she's so theatrical—I've based several performances in my career on Marian Seldes, on just her physicality.... Don't tell her [laughs]! No, she would be amused! **CHRISTINE BARANSKI**

YOU KNOW, in Chekhov, sometimes he'll have a character call another character "my little bird." I was so in love with Chekhov from the time I could read him—I suppose I started reading him when I was twelve or thirteen—I picked it up somewhere. The word, "bird" is so lovely, and it's an endearment. I used that word with my own friends, too. I don't know why, but I did it at Juilliard. I didn't hear myself do it. But, I realized, you know, they can *take you off*. My students can *do* me better than I can *do* me. Some of them are absolutely brilliant. You should hear Robin Williams *do* me. **MARIAN SELDES**

"OH, MY birds, my little birds"—Marian Seldes was great! She was like a bird herself, kind of like a flamingo. **ROBIN WILLIAMS**

Opposite, above: Marian Seldes in class with Drama Group 14

Opposite, below: Marian Seldes, 1983

Left: Marian Seldes in the new Drama Theater at Juilliard at Lincoln Center, c. 1970

VISITING ARTISTS
AND THE MASTER CLASS

Leonard Bernstein conducts a master class, March 13, 1979. Bernstein had a long-standing association with Juilliard and was involved with the faculty, students, and administration on a number of levels throughout the years.

© Beth Bergman

Opposite, above: Luciano Pavarotti master class, January 1979

Opposite, below: In 1972, opera legend Maria Callas chose twenty-six students out of three hundred to participate in a series of legendary master classes at Juilliard. In the audience were other admired artists, including Tito Gobbi, Benny Goodman, Shirley Verrett, Ben Gazzara, Lillian Gish, and Franco Zefferelli, but Callas directed her attention to the students and did not permit applause. This event became the inspiration for Terrence McNally's award-winning play *Master Class*. Juilliard Vocal Arts graduate Audra McDonald won a Tony Award in 1996 for her performance in the play.

Top left: Shirley Verrett master class, sponsored by the Marilyn Horne Foundation, January 17, 2001

Above: Conductor Herbert von Karajan with Victoria Bond, student conductor, November 1976

Left: Artur Rubinstein master class, February 12, 1975

Right: Stephen Sondheim speaking to students in the Drama Theater in 1985

Below: Choreographer and Juilliard graduate Lar Lubovitch working with students at Juilliard in 1999. Well-respected members of the dance community have visited Juilliard throughout the decades to conduct master classes, supervise the restaging of their works, create new works, and share insights and technique. Visiting artists have included Pina Bausch, Colin Connor, Donlin Foreman, Margie Gillis, Judith Jamison, Ellen Kogan, Jiri Kylian, Glen Tetley, Arlette van Boven, Paul Taylor and Hans van Manen.

Top: Playwright Arthur Miller, April 20, 1979

Above: Dame Peggy Ashcroft talks with acting teacher Marian Seldes and Drama Division director Michael Langham during a 1985 visit to Juilliard.

Above: British acting legend John Gielgud speaking to Drama Division students, December 3, 1976

WHAT IT TAKES

I REMEMBER very early on, that first semester...one of the dancers had some trauma going on in her personal life, and she came into class sort of weepy. The teacher said to all of us before she even started class, "That door, that threshold, is to this sacred place. Whatever personal traumas and problems you have going on, you leave them on the other side of the doorway. You cross that threshold pure of mind and spirit and body, prepared to work." That was pretty deep. It put me in a place where I began to work differently as a student. I began to listen much more and watch more effectively. And I credit Juilliard with really forming my eyes. **BONNIE ODA HOMSEY**

Anna Sokolow rehearsal, *The Night of the Mayas*, 1978

YOU HAVE blinders on … when you're that age. You have this star you see. If you're lucky, somebody knocks them off you and says, "Look around you." **PAULA ROBISON**

Above: The IMA News, February 28, 1942

ONE OF MY first students to get killed during [World War II] was Alex Nadel. I gave him a trumpet…. I got him a chance to go into the Navy School in Washington so he could go into a good band. But they needed him … and he went on the ship Arizona. His roommate on the boat was also a friend, a pupil of mine from Maine who kept in touch with me. It seems that one Sunday morning, the Sunday of the attack [on Pearl Harbor], they were tied up with the Nevada, I think it was. The Arizona was on the outside. As they got on shore that Sunday, Nagle realized he'd forgotten something. He told my friend, "Wait, I'm going back to get something," and as he went in a bomb dropped and killed him. He still has my trumpet down there underwater. When I went to Hawaii, I went out there—paid my respects to him, you know. **WILLIAM VACCHIANO**

ART IS A powerful thing. When you're in the midst of it, when you are young and training as an artist … either it's possible for you to stay cloistered away and strengthen your technique and your craft, and then live one day to do a very important work that may very well be politically effective, or—and those who do this are absolutely are not better or more adventurous or anything, but simply the thing they have to be true to is this other thing—say, "I have get *out there*, be in the midst of everything, be there, now."…When [the Drama] school was starting in '68 and '69, there was a lot of rhetoric on the street. There was a lot of *stuff going down*. I had a lot of friends who were into other things and they were saying, "What are you doing down there studying that stuff? You ought to be out here, doing *this* thing." And I did both things, but there was some intolerance on the part of the revolutionaries … the cultural nationalists…. Now, when the Kent State event occurred, some outside students came into Juilliard and tried to organize them in some things. And I was at this meeting [as a member of drama Group 1]—John Houseman was there, as well—and they came up with a very constructive thing to do rather than, "Don't go to classes, and tear down the building, and all that stuff." The Chamber Orchestra, I believe, played Taps and there were dancers and actors *embalmed* in makeup … laid out on the Lincoln Center Plaza …where the fountain is and down to the street. It was very, very impressive. When you heard Taps or the Requiem Mass played—it was a very powerful statement on that day for those dead at Kent State. I was very proud to be there. **STEPHEN MCKINLEY HENDERSON**

WE DIDN'T think about politics at the time, even though I would walk out of my apartment on 115th Street and run smack into the takeover at Columbia University, not having a clue as to what was going on. We had our own isolated world ... centered totally around the music.... And these days, I think young people have to be more aware of society. It's much harder to avoid. When we were kids, it didn't need to be that way. It was a different kind of society.
LEONARD SLATKIN

Above: Stephen McKinley Henderson

Right: A "lie-in" at Lincoln Center in which students and faculty protested the killings at Kent State, May 1970

SINCE THOSE first days [after the events of September 11, 2001], I have seen Juilliard and its people begin to heal, to shake off the silence so uncharacteristic of the Juilliard experience. On September 20, we gathered as a community in the Juilliard Theater to reflect on recent events through readings, dance, dramatic monologue, and music. I had been involved in planning the event, and felt a need to be close to the performance, as if the Juilliard Theater would be closed to me, as Manhattan Island had been on September 11. As a result, I watched most of the presentation from the wings. Toward the end of the gathering, the Juilliard String Quartet played the slow movement of Schubert's G Major Quartet. Hearing this group of dedicated musicians perform put much in focus for me. Juilliard is about tradition, integrity, humanity. So much was lost on September 11, but the spirit of our school and our nation came alive and grew in my mind as I heard the last chords of the quartet. On that day, I urged our students to understand that the moment will soon come when practice, rehearsals, and classes, now dwarfed by recent events, will be used for good as our young artists comfort their fellow human beings through their art in these days of sorrow and healing. **JOSEPH W. POLISI**

JUILLIARD was a very special place because of its high standards, which created in me a survival instinct. But Juilliard really made me feel, because of the competitive nature, that you were in an elite force, that you were among those commandos, that you never wanted to not be a part of that group. This is wonderful! I never want to leave that elite force of people that wants it *at the max*, not just a little bit, not just to get in there. "I want to kill"—in that sense. I want to do it the best I possibly can. Well, I got that at Juilliard. I really did. Now, were they saying that? By their very *being* and *doing*, they said that. **BILL CONTI**

TWENTY-EIGHT were chosen for drama Group 12. Who are those twenty-eight kids and where did they come from? In many cases, they're pretty much the thorough-breds of their community. They were the stars of the high-school play or the stars of the college play or maybe they'd done some acting.... You're literally throwing twenty-eight thoroughbreds into a room and saying, "Now, get along." I found, as a professional, I haven't gotten nearly close to the kind of competitive feelings I experienced at Juilliard.
KEVIN SPACEY

Left: A common sight, practicing in the halls at Juilliard. This student, Yong-Hao Pan, plays the double bass.

Opposite: Faculty review, 2000. At the end of each year, the faculty review demonstrations and works-in-progress from the various dance disciplines.

IT'S CONSTANTLY said that musicians sacrifice a great deal of their personal life for their music, and that's true. You sacrifice part of your childhood. You sacrifice part of your adolescence. You sacrifice family life when you're older—because the music does come first. **LEONARD SLATKIN**

EACH FACULTY member would comment on your work, your speech, your voice, your acting, your body, and this made people feel so vulnerable. A lot of people I don't think survived. It was very hard. After all, at that age it's hard to have a mask ripped off of you if you don't have something underneath. A lot of people were [having things] stripped away who didn't have egos hardy enough to withstand that kind of scrutiny. **CHRISTINE BARANSKI**

IT'S HARD and it's four years. The demand, every day, to be committed to every moment that you are in class is not easy. There is no way for a student to come into a class and just *wing it*. In my class you can't do that. You cannot just come in and be part of it without being fully committed to every moment of the hour-and-a-half in which we work. I'm sure every other teacher demands the same thing. We commit ourselves to the class as teachers, and we ask the same thing from the students. So class after class, day after day, makes it quite difficult. It takes a special person to be able to go through it, a special will and a special need. **MONI YAKIM**

Opposite: Juilliard students rehearsing at the school, 2000

Above: Comedy class with John Towsen and drama Group 18

Above: Eriq La Salle, Group 13, in movement class

Opposite: Eriq La Salle in movement class with Moni Yakim. After leaving Juilliard, La Salle went on to complete his training at the drama program at New York University.

I WAS TOLD I wasn't going to be asked back. At eighteen, I had a very specific game plan— I would do Juilliard for four years, and I would join The Acting Company. This was all based on seeing that photo of Keith David playing Othello [on the cover of the Drama Division brochure]. That was my world. It was truly one of the most devastating things in my life. You know, at that age, at that period, it was absolutely devastating, because I was giving everything that I had.

I saw a lot of people emotionally castrated. I saw a lot of people who came in with some very basic brilliant talent, ultimately destroyed. And I saw some people reach incredible heights and success. That's what it is. It's a balance. Some will survive and some won't.

I was very, very protective—I might not have known much going into that situation, but what I did know, I fought desperately to protect. I saw others who didn't, and it cost them. A lot of my classmates…. I don't know that they're acting anymore.

I've seen and experienced the best and worst of Juilliard—in the training I have received—the best and worst of it. You know, it's weird…at the end of the day, you'll always hear me say, "If I had to do it again, I'd do the exact same thing." It's a hell of a training. It's incredible training, but it costs you.

By no means am I depicting Juilliard as the evil big brother or anything like that, but I think that there's a balance. When I left Juilliard, I had something that very few artists had, very few actors had. I had something, particularly, that very few minority actors had, and it became a huge, huge asset. I had technique. I had incredible technique. I had a classical training.

Obviously, when you are rejected from something, your ego is just absolutely annihilated. Over the years, being kicked out of Juilliard has become a sort of badge of honor, [laughs] you know? So, for me, it's actually pretty cool. Mike Beach is my best friend and he doesn't miss an opportunity to tell someone, "You know, I graduated Juilliard. He got kicked out." [laughs] It's a running joke, now. Obviously, back at that time, phew! It wasn't a joke. It is in some ways a badge of honor for me—just as being a survivor. I held on to my gut instinct and I held on to my beliefs, and they've paid off. **ERIQ LA SALLE**

I REMEMBER the moment when I saw Eriq La Salle coming around the corner on the lot at Warner Bros. where he [was] doing *ER*—and he had just gotten this huge, huge contract. I saw him, and I put my arms around him because I remembered him coming around the corner when he got cut at Juilliard. He so wanted, clearly, to be an actor, and being at Juilliard was so important to him. Here's this young kid who was let go out of this program for what I think he has proven to be, ridiculous reasons, and he comes out crying, thinking his life is over. Now, there's like an "Eriq La Salle Wing" at Juilliard! **BRADLEY WHITFORD**

THE ONE thing I was consistently concerned about, or at least it made a good joke, was that all of the best actors had either left or got kicked out! So I was a little concerned that maybe if I stayed it meant that I would was never have a career in theater and film. **VAL KILMER**

Above: Dancer and choreographer Robert Garland during his student years at Juilliard

Below: Dance student Martha Clarke alone in a Claremont Avenue studio

BEING successful in the arts is like roulette. There are great people who have gone down and not-such-great people who've risen. But you have to *need* to take the ride to survive in it. I've had glory and I've had amazing failure, and you have to get a tough skin to survive, a really thick skin. You have to love it for the process, because you can't predict the results or how the public's going to respond or how the press is going to respond. You have to love the day-by-day work of making things…. You can't look at it like watching grass grow every day. If you don't love being there and enjoy it and love the interaction and the collaboration with your fellow artists and peers, don't do it! Because—it's often a heartache. **MARTHA CLARKE**

194

Dancer Abdur-Rahim Jackson was one of the five students featured in the *American Masters* documentary film *Juilliard*. After graduating in 2000, Jackson fulfilled his childhood dream and joined the Alvin Ailey Dance Company.

GRADUATING from Juilliard would mean a lot to everybody in my family because I would be the first one of my mother's children to graduate from college… and that would be good because I think that sets a role model for my little brothers and sisters. I wouldn't expect to be here. Black men my age are either selling drugs, dead, or in jail…and I was supposed to be in those statistics. I don't see it right now because I'm busy working, but for other people they are like "Abdur came a long way" [laughs]. People will tell you stories about me… But, it is a difference. It truly is a difference.

I think that what this experience has taught me…is that this constant struggle that I have to deal with…is a good thing. And for some reason, people think I'm strong enough to do it. So I think I can…. I know that I can deal with it! **ABDUR-RAHIM JACKSON**

Jeffrey Carlson, drama Group 30, 2000, was featured in the *American Masters* documentary *Juilliard*.

YOU GET IN here because they think you have potential…that you have something. And if you really love it everyone's fighting to be… It's not really "Am I good? Am I good?" It's not that! You just want to be able to *move* things….You want to be able to do something with what you've got. Here, I have every reason to be an artist. It's a really hard thing to remember. Because insecurities can be at full force inside this building because of the expectations that you put on yourself, and that are on you…because you want to be great! **JEFFREY CARLSON**

THE ONE tyranny you mustn't have is the tyranny of your self. You mustn't have your fears control you. You mustn't have your *wanting to have an image* control you. So I spend a lot of time getting actors to break the chains of their own tyranny so they can have the guts to survive and combat the tyranny from outside. **MICHAEL KAHN**

YOU HAVE to have the faith and the trust in them—that they're being critical for the right reasons and about the right things and that eventually it will come together for you. That can be very hard when you're in your early twenties, and you're locked in a building fourteen hours a day, and you have no other life, and it becomes so overly important to you. That's really hard. I was pretty good about that—not always, but pretty good about it.

I think that's why … you hear about students having psychologically hard times. That's a lot of it—criticism is taken too much to heart or becomes too important. Or they forget that the faculty is on your side. It can easily become an adversarial relationship. But that faculty is really on their side—it doesn't feel like that all the time. But I really believe that. **LAURA LINNEY**

SOMETIMES, when people are riding you, pushing you—not cajoling you, not comforting you, but actually challenging you … these are, in fact, the best people sometimes. These are the people who are trying to say, "I see what you have. I see your potential. But I also see what stops you from getting through." **KEVIN SPACEY**

Drama student Irving (Ving) Rhames, Group 12, in class with Marian Seldes, 1980

PRESSURE. If you can't handle it, then you don't want to aspire to be center stage. Why would you want a teacher who cannot expose you as early as possible to what center stage is like? It's one thing to be able to cope in the studio. But there are miles to go before you are center stage as a *professional*. **LEONTYNE PRICE**

Thomas Grubb, French diction and vocal literature faculty, 2000

THE STRESS? You were constantly being told everything you were doing was wrong, and if this is your only option for your career in life, you ended up feeling like, "Well, what's left if I can't do this? What's gonna be there for me after this?" That's how I felt at Juilliard—if I don't succeed there's nothing else for me to do. I have not prepared myself to do anything else because I have been in a conservatory all this time. I am not reading the great classics. I am not studying biology. I am just studying what's supposed to be my life's work and that's it. That's huge.

I had a great teacher at Juilliard named Thomas Grubb … [who] is still there. He is the French diction and vocal literature teacher. He really picked up on the fact that I liked to inhabit a song and perform a song, and he started picking things for me to do that were more suited to my personality. Instead of selecting a song that a proper twenty-one-year-old lyric soprano *should* sing, he thought, "*This* is a good one for Audra, for her spirit." That's when I finally started to find some success, find myself in opera. And I know I owe it all to him. **AUDRA McDONALD**

Audra McDonald, 1991

Omar Butler, trumpet student, practicing in his dormitory room, 2000

WHEN I came to The Juilliard School, I found my existence there, with a couple of wonderful exceptions, was pretty lonely because it meant working hard. We know that all we want to do is become artists, or become great instrumentalists, and to hone our craft. A music school of that level doesn't have to be a happy place. I don't know that finding happiness, for an artist, is what any of us consider the most important thing. For many artists (and we are a complicated lot of people), the great joy is when the music is working and coming to us. Often, our most joyous, passionate moments are on the stage or in communion with other artists having a musical experience, making a piece come to life. That's what we spend our lives trying to do. Why else would we go into a practice room and close the door and spend all those hours? It's to find our way to the truth, to find our way inside the music, to find that light—and that doesn't mean the light of fame and fortune; it means the truth of art. So, when you go to a conservatory, you have to realize that that's probably what a lot of other people around are looking for and some of them don't want…happy communion. A lot of people really want to be by themselves and work.
PAULA ROBISON

THE PRESSURE was extraordinary, and it still is extraordinary…If you go to law school or medical school and you graduate as an average lawyer or average doctor, you can still guarantee that you're gonna have a pretty decent career and a pretty decent income. But in the arts, there's really no room for that middle level of work, so students are constantly being measured against the best of the best. The performers are constantly being measured against the star artists who are traveling around the world, doing remarkable things. And for composers, my God! We're measured against Beethoven, Bach, Stravinsky, and Schoenberg…some of the most illuminating figures of human history. **EDWARD BILOUS**

I REALLY believe that Juilliard has a moral commitment to make sure that our young people get the type of education that will permit them to be effective advocates for the arts in the United States and around the world. Without focused advocacy, the arts in America will continue to be misunderstood and undersupported. **JOSEPH W. POLISI**

A concert bassoonist in addition to his career as a writer and educator, Joseph W. Polisi became president of the Juilliard School in 1984. His father, William Polisi, had been a well-known bassoonist with The New York Philharmonic, and was also on the faculty of The Juilliard School. In his convocation speech in 1999, Dr. Polisi made the following remarks: "For those of you who are new to Juilliard and those who are seasoned veterans, I'm sure you've heard the stories—most apocryphal—of how competitive this place can be. But I think you have seen, or will see, that Juilliard is a deeply supportive place dedicated to its students and the standards of the profession. In other words, as Mark Twain said of the music of Wagner, 'It's not as bad as it sounds.' "

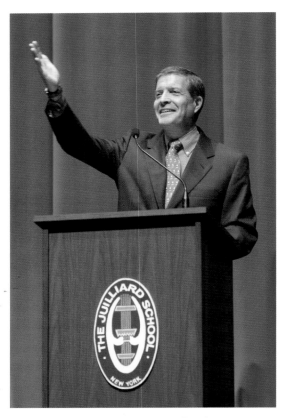

Joseph W. Polisi speaking at Juilliard Convocation, 2001

IN THE YEARS that I have observed Joseph Polisi in his role as president of the Juilliard School, it has become clear to me that he is inspired by the belief that there are two facets to the challenge of properly educating young performance artists. Because of his leadership, Juilliard addresses not only the requirement that each student be trained to his or her highest capacity in the technical aspects of a particular art form, but also the need to develop each young artist as a well-rounded individual capable of realizing his or her full potential in society, and of functioning, whenever possible, as an effective advocate for the rightful place of arts in society.

I have also had occasion to observe a gratifying level of attention on the part of the students at the Juilliard School to opportunities to share their talents with the broadest possible audience, an attention that takes them into public schools as teachers and into hospitals, nursing homes and other institutions, as performers. They are able to do so because of programs initiated by Joseph Polisi, and which have pleased me to support. Also, in his years at Juilliard, Joseph Polisi has worked diligently and purposefully to create an institution whose student body, faculty, and staff are fully reflective of the diverse makeup of our city and our nation.

In addition to technical mastery and a well-rounded education, Juilliard graduates take with them an ingrained sense of responsibility to the communities around them and an understanding of the value of the arts to their communities. Through the beliefs and actions of Juilliard's alumni, the values that Joseph Polisi has put in place at the school will influence the arts and society for generations to come. **IRENE DIAMOND**

I THINK the big difference in the school today is having the dormitory. When I was there, there was no dorm. Pianists really only knew pianists. There was very little inter-departmental mingling. Dancers stuck with themselves. The drama division did their thing. Opera did theirs. So there really wasn't any cross-fertilization of ideas or shared experience. And I really didn't like that; it was tough. You basically coexisted. That's what it felt like. And today, I spend a lot of time in the school and am quite active in the school, and it's completely different. You see the collaboration between dancers and composers and between divisions. It's fantastic. That is really the beauty of the school, and I think it's because they live together, they commune together, and that makes a big difference. **JULIE CHOI**

I THINK it's hard on some of the older faculty, probably, to realize that there are exigencies now that didn't exist in the old days. You just don't stick a kid in an ivory tower called Juilliard, and not take into consideration how he's going to eat, or how she's going to find an apartment, or that there are emotional problems to do with competition or any number of other things. It's a growing awareness, as in society in general, of how the school has to be a different kind of place. **MARY RODGERS GUETTEL**

Opposite, below: Polisi speaking with students Sheila Browne, Melvin Chin, and Aaron Flagg, who now has a leadership position in the Music Advancement Program (MAP) at Juilliard, April 1993

Above, right: Students gather for the Juilliard Jazz Picnic, May 2000.

Right: The exterior of Meredith Willson Residence Hall, which opened in 1990

EVERYDAY LIFE

THE THING that made the biggest difference to me was my friends, my colleagues, the other students who I went to school with in my class and how they influenced me. We would sit down and talk about music—intellectually stimulating conversation about music that you have with your friends. The talks that we had on orchestra break in stairway E, in the cafeteria, in the subway going to school, or walking around the neighborhood, that's where I got my stimulation...

Now, when I think back on it, when I was a student there, every single person I knew was so individual, so unique. We each had very strong opinions about everything under the sun. We were, some of us, quite rebellious and not afraid. Not nasty, but naughty.

I think that's partially the reason why I am so open about music—because of the people that I went to school with. They were all so vibrant and stimulating, and different. And yet, we had this one thing in common, this place that we went to.

NADJA SALERNO-SONNENBERG

Students on Lincoln Center Plaza, 2000

ARRIVING at Juilliard…was like arriving in the world's most phenomenal candy store, if you're a person like me who can never get enough music. The student body was so talented and, for the most part, very focused. And the faculty was this extraordinary array of the first-class people in their fields. **JAMES LEVINE**

Above: Juilliard students move into the new residence hall, October 10, 1990.

Opposite: Nora Downes, with Joseph W. Polisi, is honored at a reception marking her retirement from Juilliard in 1996. Born in County Galway, Ireland, Nora Downes came to America by herself in 1930 at the age of nineteen. When she began working at the Claremont Avenue building, in 1948, she was responsible for a variety of tasks, including cleaning the practice rooms. She recalled, "Sometimes I would hear John Browning practice, or Van Cliburn would play a little for me." After Juilliard moved to Lincoln Center, she was appointed to her post at the main security desk, where she warmly greeted every student, faculty member, and administrator with her classic Irish accent. In a 1991 interview for *The Juilliard Journal,* when asked how she felt about encountering so many famous people in the course of her Juilliard career, she replied, "They're just like ourselves. They do their job as best they've learned to do it, and then they go home. Just like ourselves."

YOU'RE talking about, for the most part, eighteen-year-old malleable minds. You're talking about people really trying to define themselves as adults. There's sexuality, there is independence from your parents, there is integration. I went to school with people who had never been around black people. I remember a guy told me the only black person he ever knew was his maid. I came from a 99 percent black environment, and now I was in a 99 percent white environment. And I'm eighteen, I'm young, I'm very impressionable. I am trying to define myself as a man…as an artist, and as a black man. **ERIQ LA SALLE**

THE FIRST person who you greeted when you walked in the Juilliard School was Nora, the gatekeeper on the first floor. She was a beautiful, wonderful Irish lady who had been there, many would say, since the school began. She's passed on now. But she took care of us. Nora would make sandwiches for us and she'd give certain students lunch or an apple. She sort of designated certain students every year who she would take care of. She was an incredibly sweet lady. **KEVIN SPACEY**

OH, SHE was a joy… Nora. She saw that everything was in order…. And then, as she got older, she was loved so much by the school that they put her at the front desk at reception. Everybody knew Nora. You wouldn't walk by her without kissing her. She was fairly insulted if you didn't. And she stayed there a long time until she became ill. She was a wonderful lady. She was really part of Juilliard. I knew her at least forty years….She was the most loved woman in the whole school.

WILLIAM VACCHIANO

NORA was there.
"How are you? Do you need money for food?"
"Oh, no, I'm fine."
"Here, son. Here's a sticky bun. Take it with you"
Nora was like that, you know.
Moments…pockets of humanity in the midst of it all.
ROBIN WILLIAMS

DURING THE Depression when money was very scarce, I received fifty dollars a month to live on—which was a lot of money. It was one big family. The school was small enough that you knew everybody, not like today with the huge enrollments. I think the enrollment was maybe a few hundred, and it was a very warm feeling. I met this clarinet player there, Josephine La Prade, and the third year I was at school, we were married. We rented an apartment on Claremont Avenue at thirty-five dollars a month. And there was a very famous restaurant on 110th Street called The Brass Rail. We used to eat there every night—thirty-five cents was a full meal. It was a great time in my life. I enjoyed it. They were the best years of my life.

WILLIAM VACCHIANO

Top: Willliam Vacchiano, while studying trumpet at the IMA, c. 1935

Above: Josephine La Prade, future wife of William Vacchiano, while a student at the IMA, c. 1930s

Opposite: The Claremont Avenue building, c. 1950

Above: Students register for class, c. 1960.

I REMEMBER the coffee shop because it was a meeting place where you could sit down and have a cup of coffee and say, "Isn't that Vincent Persichetti at the next table?" Or Roger Sessions? Or all the people there? And yes, they were there. They were just drinking a cup of coffee. I didn't know until after I was admitted to the school that you could just simply say, "Mr. Persichetti, do you mind if I sit down?" And he would say, "Yeah—what are you working on? Come, have a coffee." And you could actually pass hours with these mentors, with these incredible teachers. They were wonderful.

BILL CONTI

Above right: Music students in the cafeteria, 2000

Right: The cafeteria at Claremont Avenue, c. 1959

210

Left: Jeanne Tripplehorn and Saundra Quarterman as students at Juilliard

Below: Student borrowing scores from Juilliard Library, 2000. Juilliard's library was completely renovated in 1999 with funding from the Peter Jay Sharp Foundation. The facility is fully networked: students may use one of the nineteen public-access computers for access to library resources or plug in a laptop at one of the reading-room tables.

IN JUILLIARD—as in any college or workplace—you have your clique of people that you hang with. But the world—meaning Juilliard—really came together in the cafeteria. That's where everybody went to eat. We would see actors—now extraordinarily famous actors—coming in and out all the time, having coffee or smokes. The dancers came in and got their carrots, and smoked. They always smelled. The brass guys would hang by themselves over here, and the string players would hang over there. If you just took a look around in that room, there was an awful lot of buried talent. That's why I majored in cafeteria. I loved the cafeteria—just to look around and see everybody trying to learn their craft, and trying to mentally mess around with their colleagues. It was always a lot of fun to watch. **NADJA SALERNO-SONNENBERG**

I KNEW THAT I must have artistic potential when my beloved friend and great, great, great pianist Van Cliburn came over to speak to me in the dining room. Instrumentalists seldom had a conversation with singers. We were not quite in the *upper echelons*, I would say. **LEONTYNE PRICE**

211

THERE WAS a guy I remember named Spit Valve. We called him Spit Valve. He played the French horn. He would come into our rooms and dump his spit valve out on the floor. His spit would be all over the place. He didn't understand that we roll around on those floors. We do a lot of work on the floor. I didn't want to be rolling around in his spit! We'd constantly be in wars about space and things like that. Everyone just made fun of each other. The actors made fun of the dancers. The dancers made fun of the opera singers. The opera singers made fun of the musicians. Everyone sort of had a friendly adversarial relationship because we had to share one space.
LAURA LINNEY

THEY HAD good parties. Good parties.

When I was on jury duty the first time in New York, they asked me, "What you do?"

And I said, "I'm a teacher."

"Where?"

"Juilliard."

The case was clearly a drug case. They asked, "Have you ever been around drugs?"

And I said, "Yes, I have."

And they said "Recently?"

[And I said,] "Well, you're living in New York in 1977. You go to any party, and somebody's going to be smoking pot or doing *something*."

I did not get chosen, by the way, for that jury. But afterward, a little old lady—she must have been in her eighties—who had also been in the prospective jury pool, came up to me and said, "I want to tell you I went to Juilliard as a violinist—I graduated in 1933—and we never had that much fun at that school."
TIM MONICH

I REMEMBER stumbling into one of the rehearsal rooms late at night, trying to find a place to do a scene with my partner. And there were Franny Conroy and Bill Hurt—two of the great living American actors, right now. They were doing a scene from Ostrovsky, just on their own. I couldn't breathe, it was so amazing. And they were just nineteen. But that's very rare. You knew you were seeing something legendary. You knew that Bill was going to be one of the great, great actors. And you knew that Franny was, as well. That it was very special. **GREGORY MOSHER**

Top: Dancers in the halls between classes, 2000

Above: Drama students from Group 6, Diane Venora and Frances Conroy, in a rehearsal for Shakespeare's *A Midsummer Night's Dream*, 1974

JAZZ

IT'S VERY important that we started a jazz program at Juilliard. It's important for our school. Juilliard has a tradition that is well known. Many great musicians have come through the halls of Juilliard. Its the very best that we have to offer to the world of our arts—the American arts. It's like the New York Yankees. I mean, the level is very high, and we maintain that level. Places like Juilliard are very, very important. You can reach a situation where things of intelligence and refinement and culture can be considered *elite*, and things that are crass and ignorant can be considered *real* and *of the people*. When you begin to have the mass of the populace believing that they should strive for something that is not worth striving for, then a tremendous amount of energy goes into the worthless, and the maintenance of that which is worthless. It is a battle we all fight, even within ourselves. You have to actively pursue knowledge. It out there for you, and you *gotta* go out and get it. And you *gotta* want it. And you *gotta* keep wanting it. **WYNTON MARSALIS**

Above: Clarinetist and saxophonist Victor L. Goines, artistic director of Jazz Studies, with students. The Institute for Jazz Studies, Juilliard's newest program, began in 2001. The tuition-free, preprofessional, two-year program is a collaboration between two organizations—The Juilliard School and Jazz at Lincoln Center. The Jazz studies program has a distinguished faculty of active performers and composers who have worked with and learned from the great jazz musicians.

Opposite: Wynton Marsalis performing at an event celebrating the announcement of Juilliard's new Institute for Jazz Studies, 2000. Marsalis, the artistic director of Jazz at Lincoln Center, was a student at Juilliard, where he studied trumpet with William Vacchiano, among others. Juilliard students now study with Marsalis, and he is a member of Juilliard's board of trustees.

ONE OF my fine students who made it real big in the jazz world is Miles Davis. He was a little on the eccentric side. He would refuse to sit in a chair. He always sat on his trumpet case and he'd wear a little beanie for his lessons. But he was very conscientious about learning.... When they came to study with me—the real jazz players—I would just teach them the fundamentals from the bible—scales and arpeggios. I would train them to be *legitimate men*...because I don't know anything about jazz! **WILLIAM VACCHIANO**

Above: Miles Davis, late 1940s

Opposite: Duke Ellington in 1939 with his son, Mercer Ellington, who was enrolled in Juilliard's Diploma Trumpet program from 1938 to 1940. Mercer Ellington's daughter, Mercedes Doralyn Ellington, also studied at Juillard, and was awarded a B.S. degree in Dance in 1960.

Son Follows Father

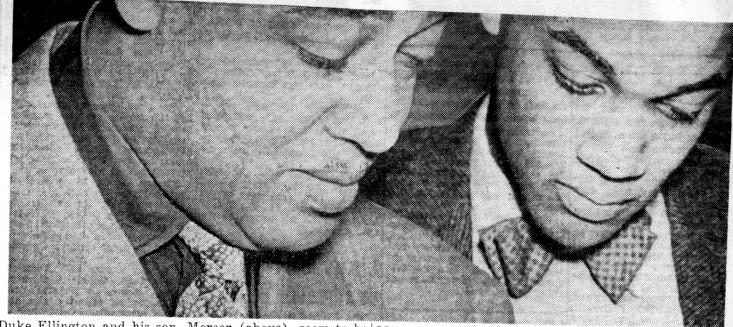

Duke Ellington and his son, Mercer (above), seem to be taking the business in hand quite earnestly, and well might they be, for it's music they're discussing. Mercer is to swing out with a band of his own in the next few days, although very little publicity is being given the venture just now. But, they do say, it will have thirteen pieces.

Mercer, a student at the Juilliard School of Music (where they don't take you unless you're good) has composed a number of pieces, some of which have been played by his father's band (which doesn't play music unless it's good).

WHEN I WAS at Juilliard, jazz in New York was certainly flourishing. One could go hear Miles Davis, Stan Getz, the Ellington band, the Basie band, or any number of names, all of whom were performing in New York. And I saw and heard them all—had great interest in it, and loved the music, of course. Great progress was being made at that time in our search for a national voice. We still had to some degree a cultural inferiority complex that lingered in North America, in the world of music and opera. I was infatuated, as many young people were, with the popular music of that day. It was the end of the great period of American songwriting, that incredibly rich three or four decades that had produced Cole Porter, Gershwin, Jerome Kern, Ellington, and the others that we lauded as our own. Social forces—immigration, wars, depressions—conspired to produce this wonderful music. Looking back, we now realize it was a great period of artistic energy, not seriously recognized at the time by the academic world, and probably missed by Juilliard also, at least in terms of what was on the curriculum. We've come a long way in our acceptance of diversity, socially and musically. I think of Bernstein, who spoke of all the parts of music as forming one body, one corpus, one organic, living entity, teaching us a lot about acceptance. **JOHN WILLIAMS**

THE BIG PICTURE

OUR GREATEST accomplishment in the four years that they spend here is that we push them to a bridge that they walk over and that is the bridge to the stage. What transforms the wonderful dancer in a studio, the technical dancer, the dancer who bounds about, is a pleasure to watch. How do we transform that dancer into a performer, an artist who can repeat perhaps the same role again and again and again and yet make it seem like it's the first time it's happening? I believe the answer is *a technique*, and we approach it through repertory classes in which they learn to deal with masterworks of the past and present, which makes them search within for subtleties—the nuances of the use of weight, the intensity of the focus. **BENJAMIN HARKARVY**

Class of 2000 posing for a graduation photograph at Juilliard

I DON'T THINK it's enough to just play your instrument really well. You not only have to be a good performer, but you also have to be an advocate of arts. You have to know where your discipline fits within the context of the overall American culture. Juilliard students, in fact all performing artists, are ambassadors traveling around the world, resonating and communicating with audiences. It's not enough just to stand up and play, you have to know where the music that you're playing fits into the bigger picture. **EDWARD BILOUS**

YOU DON'T graduate from Juilliard as a finished actor. You graduate knowing how much there is to know, which is what any good education teaches one. **KEVIN KLINE**

Above: Doris Humphrey and Frederick Prausnitz face the stage, Claremont Avenue.

Below: Vocal Arts student Sarah Wolfson was featured in the *American Masters* documentary *Juilliard*, 2000.

TRADITION! You were always aware that you were a part of this gigantic, bigger-than-life tradition at The Juilliard School—that you were bathed in kind of a rarified light, you felt special, and that going into the outside world would inevitably be challenging and difficult. But having this experience made me feel I'd been through some incredible cathartic learning experience—it gave me an edge and made me feel a little bit more ready for my world.

The kind of music I was so immersed in and really loved at the time I was at Juilliard has not left me, whatsoever. Doing the music for *The X-Files*—I've been able to draw from so much of that early experience at Juilliard and my involvement with new music, experimental music, electronic music. **MARK SNOW**

WHEN I THINK about Juilliard in the context of Lincoln Center, I think about my first year here when I had my first voice lessons. I looked out my window in my studio where I was working with my teacher—and there is the Met, and there is the State Theater, and there is Avery Fisher Hall! You can't help but make some sort of parallel, thinking, "Here I am right now, but will I be there in five, ten, fifteen, twenty years?" It's not necessarily in the context of *my* future, but just the historical presence of Lincoln Center and the people who have been at this school! I remember as a freshman, we would always say, "Oh yea, Leontyne Price took a breath of this air! Wynton Marsalis was taught by my ear-training teacher, and I am sure he went through the same things that I went through!" So it's more than just, "I'm gonna be this big star at Lincoln Center!" It's that you already feel you are a part of a world that has happened and is happening around you. **SARAH WOLFSON**

ULTIMATELY, in music, you're only happy if you wind up doing what you want to do. So, I say try to figure out early on what you're willing to have as your career. If you say to yourself, "Okay, I'm going to be the next Horowitz, the next Heifetz, the next Leontyne Price," it's nice to believe that, but then try to put a dose of reality in it. Check in with your teachers about it. Try to keep an even keel as to what you can really accomplish. To some people, there are no boundaries. Other people have aspirations and never attain them, and have miserable lives.

It's mostly about making a good life for yourself. Making music, in whatever form you do, is a way of giving pleasure and joy to so many.

You have to remember always, when you go to Juilliard or any school, why you are going there. What's going to be your end result? Will you remember what it was like to be inspired by music, and will you keep that for the rest of your life? If you don't, then you shouldn't be there.
LEONARD SLATKIN

WHEN YOU'RE sitting at the piano and you're having a good time, it's about as good as it gets; I don't think there's anything much better. Well, that and a Diet Coke combined would be the ultimate. But let's not go crazy, you know? **MARVIN HAMLISCH**

Peter Schickele, c. 1991. The directions Juilliard students have taken their training and talents show infinite variety. Peter Schickele is a musician, composer, and satirist who broke through the wall of classical music into the wide-ranging world of entertainment and spectacle. At Juilliard, he studied with Vincent Persichetti and William Bergsma and served on the faculty in 1961. He is widely known as creator of the popular but imaginary composer P.D.Q. Bach, whose "work" was first performed in 1959 at Juilliard and the Aspen Music Festival, and introduced to the general public in April 1965 at New York's Town Hall. Numerous recordings followed.

WE KEEP asking them for total investment of self. I think that is what eventually produces the performer who is deeply moving. We can't explain why that person is so moving, but there's something about that person that seems so totally invested, that the moment of *their* moving and *our* watching are one, and they are making our life better in that moment. **BENJAMIN HARKARVY**

Members of the Juilliard Dance Ensemble perform Martha Graham's *Diversion of Angels*, with music by Norman Dello Joio, 1968

THE MORE you get away from school—as you're out of it year after year after year—the importance of it, which is profound, takes an appropriate place in your life. For a while, that's all you can think about. That's all you are. You're just a Juilliard student. Then, as the years roll by, it has a very nice, significant place. But it's not everything that you are. **LAURA LINNEY**

A Juilliard Dance Ensemble performance of Doris Humphrey's 1947 work *Day On Earth*, with music by Aaron Copland, 1990

Kelsey Grammer and Harriet Harris, drama Group 6, in a rehearsal project, *The Seagull*, by Anton Chekhov, 1975

THIS WHOLE question of *an acting school* is a difficult question, because it's worse than law school. It's worse than the line from Houseman's movie, *Paper Chase*—"Look to your left, look to your right. Four years from now, one of you won't be here"—which his character says to the freshman law class. Because [with acting school] if you look to your left and your left and your left, and your left, and your right, and your right, and your right, and your right, they aren't going to be there. They may make it through school, but they're not going to be working. It poses a curious dilemma for the schools, because how would you even know which kids to accept into the program when only four kids are going to make it every year! So you go through the process, you choose your twenty every year, and the faculty knows perfectly well that most of them won't make it. And no one's ever been able to solve this problem. **GREGORY MOSHER**

THE VALUE that I think the training has brought, in my own case, to the sitcom *Frasier* especially, is the comfort with language that is result of the education we got. There's a sense of imbuing the words with a size that makes them sort of resonate with importance, and that serves the sitcom format really well, because it's slightly elevated in style. And if I learned anything at Juilliard, it's to elevate your style! If Frasier could have gone to Juilliard he would have been very happy. There is something about being able to speak well that simply *reeks* of education. You just assume a person is educated who speaks well. I think it's a great lesson in terms of that character, Frasier. Certainly my training at Juilliard has fleshed him out considerably. **KELSEY GRAMMER**

PERFORMERS are addicts. They need that applause. Maybe that's what you miss when you are in a conservatory studying, that no one's there applauding. They are going, "Okay, this was wrong. This was wrong. This was wrong. And you have to work on this that and the other." So when you do finally start to get the benefit of performing, the applause and the appreciation, the communion with the audience, *helps*. **AUDRA MCDONALD**

Lisa Gay Hamilton in *Infinity House*, 1988

THE THINGS that [the teachers give you], they stay with you. They're in your memory—they're in your body memory. That's why, when I did that thing in the middle of *The Bird Cage*, that history of dance, that really quick pop—it was like seeing all the dancers, but also remembering some of those movement classes. They're in my memory bank. **ROBIN WILLIAMS**

I WAS IN a production of *The Wood Demon* that Frank Hauser directed, in which I played Val's [Val Kilmer's character's] father—a big, bearded Russian character. *Wood Demon* is actually the first version of Chekhov's *Uncle Vanya*. That, for me, was a great experience—being able to suddenly find myself with a fourth-year class, doing a main-stage production. I actually got my first manager out of that production. **KEVIN SPACEY**

BOTTOM LINE, I wouldn't be here today if it weren't for Juilliard. I'd go back in a second. I'd go through the exact same experience without question—primarily because I am a trained actor. I walk into a room, maybe not particularly confident, but knowing that I have the skills to do that role. Why do I have the skills? Because I went to Juilliard. Because I had Liz Smith, because I had Robert Williams, because I had John Stix, because I had…all the other teachers. **LISA GAY HAMILTON**

Val Kilmer and Kevin Spacey in *The Wood Demon*, 1981

Opposite, above: James Levine, at age thirteen, with Van Cliburn, 1956

Opposite, below: Flutist Paula Robison, c. 1963, her last year as a student at Juilliard

Left: Hugh Wolff conducts the Juilliard Orchestra in its final Avery Fisher concert of the 2000–2001 season, April 3, 2001, in a performance of Shostakovich's Concerto No. 1 in A Minor for Violin and Orchestra, Op. 99, featuring student violinist Misha Vitenson. The program also included Shostakovich's Symphony No. 9 in E-flat Major, Op. 70, and Stravinksy's *Symphony of Psalms*. The Juilliard Choral Union joined the orchestra for the latter.

I WAS PROBABLY one of the rare birds at Juilliard who chose to go a different route. I could imagine doing something else, and I knew that I was surrounded 99 percent by people who couldn't imagine or fathom doing anything else. This is their life, they lived and breathed the stuff—and I could! That's when I knew I needed to move on. Thinking about what to do next was definitely a challenge because you get accustomed to being surrounded by performance or achievement at a certain level, and it was hard to replicate that. Very hard. And I was lucky. **JULIE CHOI**

I BELIEVE that getting somewhere is 65 percent drive and 35 percent talent, if my arithmetic comes out right! You could have tons of talent, but if you don't have the inborn genetic grit to keep being slapped in the face with a wet fish and just keep on going and plug, you probably won't get anywhere. The world is probably full of people who are extremely talented and lack that other element called *drive*. Once you have that, I think all you have to do is keep going. And I think luck has very little to do with it.

MARY RODGERS GUETTEL

IT IS ALL around Juilliard, the idea of greatness and excellence and seeing people striving for the very, very highest. Many of them succeed, and enough of them get far enough that they can take the very best kind of equipment with them in their lives no matter where they wind up, no matter what they wind up doing with the music, dance, or theater training they've gotten there! So, even if they don't stay in New York and aren't in a Broadway show, maybe they'll be in a regional theater, maybe they will be teaching, or maybe they'll be in a small town in a beautiful part of the country or the world. They will always have with them this greatness that they received from their masters in this master place. **PAULA ROBISON**

Above: Juilliard's Tenth Annual Irene Diamond Concert featured faculty member and Juilliard alumnus Bruce Brubaker, violinist Joel Smirnoff, and Juilliard student composers and musicians, October 23, 2001, Alice Tully Hall. Pictured are Bruce Brubaker, violinist Joel Smirnoff, violist Richard O'Neill, and cellist Soo R. Bae, performing Brahms's Piano Quartet No. 3 in C Minor, Op. 60. The program also included two commissioned works by Juilliard student composers Nico Muhly and Kati Agocs, as well as two works by Philip Glass.

Opposite: Leontyne Price

NOTES

Numbers preceding entries refer to page numbers.

24: Excerpted from an unpublished memoir by Juilliard alumnus and piano faculty member Josef Raieff, of his life in music and at Juilliard.

52–57: Listed below is a chronology of the membership of the Juilliard String Quartet:

JSQ I, 1946–55: Robert Mann, Violin I; Robert Koff, Violin II; Raphael Hillyer, Viola; Arthur Winograd, Cello. *JSQ II, 1955–58:* Mann, Violin I; Koff, Violin II; Hillyer, Viola; Claus Adam, Cello. *JSQ III, 1958–66:* Mann, Violin I; Isidore Cohen, Violin II; Hillyer, Viola; Adam, Cello. *JSQ IV, 1966–69:* Mann, Violin I; Earl Carlyss, Violin II; Hillyer, Viola; Adam, Cello. *JSQ V, 1969–74:* Mann, Violin I; Carlyss, Violin II; Samuel Rhodes, Viola; Adam, Cello. *JSQ VI, 1974–86:* Mann, Violin I; Carlyss, Violin II; Rhodes, Viola; Joel Krosnick, Cello. *JSQ VII, 1986–97:* Mann, Violin I; Joel Smirnoff, Violin II; Rhodes, Viola; Krosnick, Cello. *JSQ VIII, 1997–present:* Smirnoff, Violin I; Ronald Copes, Violin II; Rhodes, Viola; Krosnick, Cello.

103: Excerpted from Peter Mennin's commencement address at Juilliard, May 31, 1963.

123: Excerpted from a speech by John Houseman at Juilliard, October 4, 1967.

126: Michel Saint-Denis quoted in John Houseman's convocation speech at Juilliard, September 24, 1968.

133: Excerpted from an interview with John Houseman by Ross Crystal on *Panorama*, February 22, 1983, WTTG-TV Channel 5, Washington, D.C.

140–41: Still video-images of a piano audition and drama audition at Juilliard drawn from the *American Masters* program *Juilliard*.

187: Excerpted from "Reflections on Loss and Healing," by Joseph W. Polisi, published in *The Juilliard Journal* (October 2001): 17, no. 2.

202: From an unpublished appreciation of Joseph W. Polisi by philanthropist Irene Diamond.

211: Below are notes on Juilliard's Library/Archives provided by Jane Gottlieb, Juilliard's Associate Vice President for Library and Information Resources:

In 1986 (the year Jane Gottlieb arrived at Juilliard), there was one small room within the library that housed archival materials. This room contained school catalogues from the earliest years, a full run of concert programs, thousands of photographs of dance, drama, and opera productions, hundreds of biographical files, and more than sixty scrapbooks documenting school activities, as well as the careers of Juilliard's students, faculty, and administrators. All of these materials have now been fully processed, catalogued, and preserved and are safely housed in the library's climate-controlled Peter Jay Sharp Special Collections Room.

The scrapbooks begin with the earliest years of the Institute of Musical Art and cover activities through the late 1950s. They are in remarkably good condition, given their acidic contents. They have been microfilmed for long-term preservation, but it is still much more rewarding to page through the original scrapbooks rather than look at the film. There are handwritten comments on many of the pages, and one gets an immediate sense of the care with which staff members documented Juilliard's early history. There appears to have been a self-conscious recognition of the major role that the institution would play in the cultural life of the nation and the world.

Juilliard's library collection of more than one hundred thousand items contains many other riches, including a large collection of original manuscripts and first editions. Rudolf E. Schirmer, son of Gustav Schirmer, founder of the famous G. Schirmer publishing house, donated the original Institute of Musical Art library, a gift that included many rare printed editions. In 1905, these scores were part of IMA's general circulating library and could be checked out by students and faculty. Today, these rare editions are part of the Peter Jay Sharp Special Collections and may only be used for special study. Juilliard has also received significant gifts of original manuscript scores, among them two songs by Johannes Brahms, a large collection of manuscripts by the Belgian violinist-composer Eugène Ysaÿe, and manuscripts of works commissioned by Juilliard, including works by Leonard Bernstein, Milton Babbitt, Elliott Carter, Aaron Copland, David Diamond, Darius Milhaud, George Rochberg, William Schuman, and Roger Sessions.

CHRONOLOGY

1905 The Institute of Musical Art (IMA) opens in the former Lenox Mansion on Fifth Avenue and 12th Street in New York City. IMA was established by Frank Damrosch, Music Supervisor for New York City's Public Schools and godson of Franz Liszt, with funding provided by philanthropist James Loeb. In its first year of existence, enrollment rose from 281 at the opening to more than 450 by the end of the academic year.

1910 The new IMA building, designed by architect Donn Barber, opens at 120 Claremont Avenue in the Morningside Heights area of New York City, November 5.

1916 The Preparatory Center (later the Pre-College Division) opens, offering special training to talented young musicians.

1919 Wealthy textile merchant Augustus Juilliard dies, April 25. His will leaves approximately $15 million for the development of music in the United States. It is the largest single bequest of its kind at the time.

1920 The Juilliard Musical Foundation is established.

1922 *The Baton*, a monthly magazine published by the Institute of Musical Art, begins publication (1922–32).

1924 The Juilliard Graduate School (JGS) is founded to help worthy students acquire a complete musical education, tuition free; it opens in the former Vanderbilt guest house at 49 East 52nd Street.

1926 The Juilliard School of Music is created through a merger of the Institute of Musical Art and the Juilliard Graduate School, October 21. The two schools share a president and board of trustees but retain separate deans and distinct identities.

1927 Pianist and composer Ernest Hutcheson is named dean of the Juilliard Graduate School.

1928 John Erskine, Columbia University Professor, best-selling author, and amateur musician, is appointed the first president of the Juilliard School of Music (1928–37).

1929 Performances of Engelbert Humperdinck's *Hansel and Gretel* by the Juilliard Graduate School mark the beginning of advanced training in opera, December 24–28. Conductor Albert Stoessel is appointed the first director of the opera department (1929–43).

1930 The Bachelor of Music Education degree program is established; it is changed to the Bachelor of Science in Music program in 1934.

1931 The Juilliard Graduate School moves to a new building on Claremont Avenue, adjacent to the IMA building. To mark the occasion, Leopold Stokowski conducts the combined orchestras of the Institute of Musical Art and the Juilliard Graduate School on November 7, and Sergei Rachmaninoff presents a solo recital on November 12.

1932 The Juilliard Summer School holds its first session. The program, directed by George A. Wedge, is in existence until 1952.

1933 The Extension Division (now Evening Division) opens, January 30.

1937 Ernest Hutcheson is appointed president of the Juilliard School of Music (1937–45).

1938 The Master of Science in Music degree program is instituted.

1944 Juilliard publishes the first of three issues of the *VVV News*, a newsletter for alumni serving in the armed forces (1944–45).

1945 Composer William Howard Schuman, winner of the first Pulitzer Prize for Music, is appointed president of the Juilliard School of Music (1945–61). Among his many accomplishments as president are the complete merger of IMA and JGS, the establishment of the Literature and Materials of Music program, the Juilliard String Quartet, and the Dance Division.

1946 The Institute of Musical Art and the Juilliard Graduate School completely merge to form a single institution.

The Juilliard String Quartet is established under the leadership of violinist Robert Mann. Its first members are Mann and Robert Koff, violins; Raphael Hillyer, viola; and Arthur Winograd, cello.

1947 The innovative Literature and Materials of Music curriculum is inaugurated. Schuman's L&M program advocates teaching the elements of music through first-hand study of musical compositions, rather than through a standard text. It has a profound impact on music theory curriculums in colleges and universities throughout the United States. *The Juilliard Report on Teaching the Literature and Materials of Music* is published by W. W. Norton in 1953.

1951 Juilliard's Dance Division is established under the direction of Martha Hill (1951–85).

1956 Juilliard celebrates its fiftieth anniversary season with a Festival of American Music, February 10–24. Most of the works performed are commissioned by the Juilliard Musical Foundation for the anniversary season. Commissioned composers include Roger Sessions, Peter Mennin, William Bergsma, Vincent Persichetti, Roy Harris, Vittorio Giannini, and Walter Piston.

1957 Aaron Copland's *Piano Fantasy*, also commissioned for the School's fiftieth anniversary, is premiered by William Masselos, October 25.

Juilliard accepts an invitation to join Lincoln Center for the Performing Arts as its educational constituent.

1958 Van Cliburn, a Juilliard piano student studying under Rosina Lhévinne, wins first place in the first Tchaikovsky competition in Moscow, making the name Juilliard known worldwide. He is welcomed back to New York with a ticker-tape parade.

1961 William Schuman is named president of Lincoln Center for the Performing Arts, Inc., September 12. His appointment is effective January 1, 1962.

1962 Composer Peter Mennin assumes Juilliard presidency, November 1. He serves until his death in 1983. Mennin oversees the school's move to Lincoln Center, establishes the Drama Division, the Juilliard American Opera Center (now the Juilliard Opera Center), and the Doctor of Musical Arts program.

1963 Bachelor of Music (BM) and Bachelor of Fine Arts degrees are instituted.

1966 Doctor of Musical Arts degree program is established.

1968 The Drama Division is established under the direction of John Houseman (1968–76) with Michel Saint-Denis as consultant.

1969 The school's name is changed to "The Juilliard School" to reflect its broadened mission in educating musicians, dancers, and actors.

Juilliard moves to its present home at Lincoln Center in a building designed by Pietro Belluschi, Eduardo Catalano, and Helge Westermann. It is a modern five-story structure with twenty-eight classrooms, fifteen two-story rehearsal studios, eighty-four practice rooms, and thirty-five teaching studios, housing more than two hundred Steinway pianos and a large permanent collection of other instruments.

A gala concert in Alice Tully Hall with soprano Leontyne Price, pianist John Browning, and the Juilliard Orchestra conducted by Alfred Wallenstein celebrates Juilliard's Lincoln Center opening, October 5.

1970 Juilliard's new American Opera Center presents its first production in the Juilliard Theater, Igor Stravinsky's *A Rake's Progress*, conducted by Erich Leinsdorf, April 23.

1971 Maria Callas presents the first of her renowned Juilliard master classes, October 11.

1972 The first class of Drama Division students (Group 1) graduates and forms The Acting Company with John Houseman.

1976 Alan Schneider is appointed director of the Drama Division (1976–79).

1979 Michael Langham is appointed director of the Drama Division (1979–92).

1983 Peter Mennin dies, June 17.

1984 Joseph W. Polisi, author, scholar, administrator, and performing bassoonist, is appointed Juilliard's sixth president. Polisi goes on to oversee the establishment of new student services and alumni programs, educational outreach programs, a revised curriculum with new emphasis on humanities and liberal arts education, and the development of interdisciplinary programs to foster greater interaction among the school's divisions.

1985 Muriel Topaz is appointed director of the Dance Division (1985–92).

Juilliard's eightieth anniversary is celebrated with a "Live from Lincoln Center" broadcast, October 5.

The Juilliard Journal begins publication.

The first annual Focus! Festival of new music is presented.

1986   The Juilliard Orchestra presents its first performance in Avery Fisher Hall, October 10.

1987   The School awards its first honorary degrees at commencement to Martha Hill, John Houseman, Leontyne Price, Itzhak Perlman, Mrs. John D. Rockefeller III, and William Schuman.

The Juilliard Orchestra tours six Asian countries, becoming the first American conservatory orchestra to visit China.

The American Brass Quintet is appointed resident brass ensemble.

1989   The New York Woodwind Quintet is appointed resident wind ensemble.

The Community Performance Fellowship Program is established to bring performances by Juilliard School students to metropolitan-area health care facilities.

1990   Juilliard's first student housing, the Meredith Willson Residence Hall, opens in the Samuel B. and David Rose Building at Lincoln Center.

The Music Advancement Program (MAP) is established for musical training of African-American, Latino, and Native American students from New York City schools.

1992   Michael Kahn is appointed director of the Drama Division (1992–present).

Benjamin Harkarvy is appointed director of the Dance Division (1992–2002).

1993   The Lila Acheson Wallace American Playwrights Program is reconstituted under the codirectorship of John Guare and Terrence McNally; Marsha Norman and Christopher Durang become codirectors the following year.

1994   The Drama Division celebrates its twenty-fifth anniversary with a gala program written by Wendy Wasserstein and Christopher Durang. Among the featured alumni performers are Christine Baranski, Kevin Kline, Patti LuPone, and Kevin Spacey.

1995   *The Juilliard Music Adventure*, an interactive CD-ROM product for teaching elements of music to children, is published in cooperation with Theatrix Interactive, Inc.

The Andrew W. Mellon Foundation Directing Program (later to become the Artists Diploma Program for Theater Directors) is instituted by Michael Kahn, JoAnne Akalaitis, and Garland Wright.

1996   Juilliard celebrates the fiftieth anniversary of the Juilliard String Quartet with commissioned works by Milton Babbitt and David Diamond.

1999   Juilliard receives the National Medal of Arts from President William Clinton, September 29 for "preeminence in arts education." The citation reads: "This renowned conservatory has trained many of the world's most talented performers of music, dance, and drama. Through free performances and by bringing its works to hospitals, nursing homes, hospices, and schools, Juilliard has strived to make the arts accessible to all."

Juilliard announces a $100 million capital campaign (later raised to $150 million) for scholarship assistance, faculty advancement, educational development, commissioning projects, and building maintenance.

Juilliard's Lila Acheson Wallace Library undergoes major renovation to create networked reading rooms and the environmentally secure Peter Jay Sharp Special Collections Room for storage of the school's distinguished collection of rare materials.

2001   The Juilliard Institute of Jazz Studies is established for advanced training of jazz musicians. Victor L. Goines is named the first director of jazz studies.

2002   Following the death of Benjamin Harkarvy in March, ballet master, artistic director, and master teacher Lawrence Rhodes is appointed artistic director of Juilliard's Dance Division, July 1.

Juilliard begins preparations for its 2005/2006 centennial.

INDEX

PHOTOGRAPH CREDITS

The authors and publisher wish to thank the individuals who generously provided photographs, and all those at libraries, museums, institutions, organizations, and agencies—especially The Juilliard School Library/Archives—who provided photographs and other illustrations.

© Charles Abbott: 74 top, 164, 144 top
AP/Wide World Photos: 62 top right, 74 bottom, 102–3, 112 top
© Richard Beeson: 67
© Beth Bergman: 38–39, 41 top, 181 top left,
© Beth Bergman 1972, 1995: 180 bottom
Karen Bernstein: 198 top
Raimondo Borea photograph © Phyllis Gilbert Borea: 133
Thomas Bouchard photograph of Martha Hill © Diane Bouchard: 78
Anthony Colantonio: 63 bottom left and top right
© 1957 by The Aaron Copland Fund for Music, Inc. Copyright Renewed. Boosey & Hawkes, Inc., Sole Publisher & Licensee. Reprinted by Permission: 51
© CORBIS/Frank Driggs: 216
© Educational Broadcasting Corporation 2000: 140, 141 top right, left and bottom
Courtesy of the George Mason University Libraries, Federal Theatre Project Photograph Collection, Special Collections and Archives: 124–25
© Robert Alan Gold: 122–23, 126 top and bottom, 127, 128 top right and bottom left, 129, 146 bottom, 160, 167 top, 177
© Diane Gorodnitzki: jacket spine fourth from top, 11, 130 bottom, 131 right, 134 top, 136, 150 top, center, and bottom, 153 top left, 213 bottom left, center, and right, 224
© Henry Grossman: 40 top left, 57, 58, 88 top, 200–201
© Erich Hartmann/Magnum Photos: 56 bottom
Courtesy of the Harvard University Archives: 17
Richard Herskovitz: 91 top

© Hatice-Nazan Isik 1995: 66 bottom
Courtesy of The Juilliard School Drama Division: 152, 153 right

The Juilliard School Library/Archives: 16, 18 bottom left, 19, 20–21, 22–23, 24 top left and top right, 25, 26–27 center, 29, 39 top left, 40 top right, 46 top, 49, 52, 53, 55, 60 left and right, 68, 69 bottom, 70, 117 top, 80, 98, 99 bottom left, 101 top left and center, 137, 162 bottom, 171 bottom left, top right and bottom right, 186, 187 right.
   Stephen Aaron: 154; David Archer: 206; String Quartet No. 3 By Elliott Carter Copyright © 1973 by Associated Music Publishers, Inc. (BMI) International Copyright Secured. All Rights Reserved. Reprinted by Permission: 110 right; Radford Bascome: 86, 168 top, 220 top; Courtesy of Hal Bergsohn: jacket spine second from top; Ed Carswell/Graphic House Inc.: 118 bottom right; Conway Studios: jacket spine fifth from top and 105; Eileen Darby/Graphic House Inc.: 46 bottom; Gerard Studio NYC, Herbert Spencer Inc.: 109; Boris Goldenberg: 73; Samuel H. Gottscho photograph courtesy of Laurie Schleisner: 40 bottom; Graphic House Inc.: 166 bottom; Vose Greenough: 210 bottom right; Philippe Halsman © Halsman Estate: jacket spine eighth from top; Impact Photos Inc.: 32, 108 bottom left, 162 top, 172, 208; Louisa Johnson: 138 bottom left; Juilliard Drama Division: 152, 153 bottom; Irving Kaufman Studios: 161; Maria Metzger: 108 top; Gili Melamed-Lev: 203 bottom; Courtesy Musical America Archives: 28; Musical Courier: 27 bottom right; Photographs by Milton Oleaga © The Juilliard School: 79, 116–17, 222; Ray Pierce: 50; Jane Rady: 168 bottom; Elizabeth Sawyer: 170, 171 top left and center left; Susan Schiff: 89 bottom; Jenna Soleo: 182 left; Herbert Spencer Inc.: 51 top, 104; Lisl Steiner: 43; Ezra Stoller © ESTO: 99 top right; Martha Swope/TimePix: 223; Trio Press Inc.: 33 bottom, 54; Harvey Weber/Graphic House Inc.: 42; Washington,

D.C. Weekly Afro-American photograph courtesy of the Afro-American Newspaper Company of Baltimore Inc.: 217; Whitestone Photo/Heinz H. Weissenstein All rights reserved: 181 bottom, 183 bottom right; Zindman/Fremont, New York, copy prints of photographs and other archival material in The Juilliard School Library/Archives: 16, 18 bottom left, 19, 20–21, 24 top left, 26-27, 27 right, 28, 29, 39 top, 46 top, 51 bottom, 53, 56 bottom, 60 left and right, 101 top left and center, 110 right, 123, 137, 138 bottom, 171 bottom left, top right, bottom right, 186 and 187 right, 217, Juilliard Milestones photographs in front endpaper: IMA entrance Claremont Avenue building, IMA opera students; in back endpaper: Concert program, Joseph W. Polisi and the Crown Prince of Japan

© Clemens Kalischer: 227 top
© Jessica Katz: jacket spine sixth from top and 120–21, 130 top right, 131 bottom left, 135 top and bottom, 138 top, 139, 142–43, 144, 145 top and bottom, 146 top right, 147, 148 top and bottom, 149, 151 top and bottom, 155, 175, 176 top and bottom, 191, 192, 193, 197, 211 top, 225 bottom
Daniel E. Lewis: 4, 84, 173 and jacket spine third from top, 209 bottom right, Lincoln Center for the Performing Arts Inc. Archives: 94–95, 96, 97, Alex V. Sobolewski photograph of Luciano Berio courtesy of Lincoln Center for the Performing Arts Inc. Archives: 113
© Nan Melville: 2–3, 33 top, 61 center right, 69 top, 91 bottom, 92–93, 112 bottom, 169, 203 top, 214, 215, 228
© Alfredo Miccoli: jacket front, 76–77, 156 top, 158 top and bottom, 159 top and bottom, 188, 189, 190, 195, 196, 199, 204–5, 210 top right, 211 bottom, 212–13 top, 218–19, 220 bottom
Museum of the City of New York Theatre Collection: jacket spine top, 18 top
The New York Herald Tribune: 123 top

The New York Public Library, Astor, Lenox and Tilden Foundations, Milstein Division of United States History, Local History and Genealogy: 12–13
The New York Times: 14 top and center, 24 top right, 41 bottom, 101 right, 132, Neal Boenzi/The New York Times: 71, Fred R. Conrad/The New York Times: 202 bottom, James Estrin/The New York Times: 134 bottom
Roger Phenix: 63 bottom right
Photofest: 87
Carol Pratt: 72 bottom right
© Peter Schaaf: 9, 30–31, 34, 36–37, 44–45, 47 top left, top right, bottom left, 56 top, 59, 62 bottom left, 64, 66 top, 75 top and bottom, 81, 88 bottom, 89 top, 106–7, 111 left and right, 114–15, 119, 156 bottom, 157, 163 bottom, 165, 174, 178–79, 180 top, 181 top right, 182 left, 183 top and bottom left, 184–85, 202 top, 221, 226, jacket spine ninth from top and 229
Courtesy of G. Schirmer, Inc. Archives: 48
© 2002 Rahav Segev/Photopass.com: jacket back
© Steve J. Sherman: 35, 47 bottom right, 118 top
Martha Swope/TimePix photograph courtesy of School of American Ballet: 100
TWU Photograph by Tom Matthews: 207

Personal Collection of Martha Clarke, photograph courtesy of Martha Clarke: 194 bottom
Personal Collection of Dorothy DeLay, photograph courtesy of Dorothy DeLay and Barbara Sand: 61 top left
Personal Collection of Robert Garland, photograph courtesy of Robert Garland: 194 top
Personal Collection of Marvin Hamlisch, photograph courtesy of Marvin Hamlisch: 61 bottom left
Personal Collection of Benjamin Harkarvy, Kenn Duncan photograph courtesy of Benjaman Harkarvy and the Pennsylvania Ballet: 90 right
Personal Collection of Solveig Lund

Madsen, photograph courtesy of Donna Kline: 163 top
Personal Collection of Bruce Marks, Daniel Entin photograph courtesy of Bruce Marks and Daniel Entin: 90 left
Personal Collection of Audra McDonald, photograph courtesy of Audra McDonald: 198 bottom
Personal Collection of Stephen McKinley Henderson, Joe Terrell photograph courtesy of Stephen McKinley Henderson: 186 right
Personal Collection of Paula Robison, Christian Steiner photograph courtesy of Paula Robison and Christian Steiner: jacket spine seventh from top and 227 bottom
Personal Collection of Muriel Topaz, M. David Varon photograph courtesy of Muriel Topaz: 85
Personal Collection of Ellen Taaffe Zwilich, photographs courtesy of Ellen Taaffe Zwilich: 110 top left, 167 bottom
Personal Collection of William Vacchiano, photographs courtesy of William Vacchiano: 209 top left (DeBarron photograph) and bottom left

Juilliard Milestones
Front endpaper, left to right:
[Damrosch] Museum of the City of New York Theatre Collection, [IMA Entrance, Claremont Avenue building] The Juilliard School Library/Archives, [IMA preparatory students] The Juilliard School Library/Archives, [Orchestra class, 1927] Empire Flashlight Co. photograph courtesy of The Juilliard School Library/Archives, [IMA opera students] The Juilliard School Library/Archives, [Summer school students] The Juilliard School Library/Archives, [Martha Hill and colleagues] Susan Schiff photograph courtesy of The Juilliard School Library/Archives, [Festival of British Music production] The Juilliard School Library/Archives,

Back endpaper, left to right:
[John Houseman] The Juilliard School Library/Archives, [Concert program] The Juilliard School Library/Archives, [The School for Scandal production] Diane Gorodnitzki, [Bradley Whitford, backstage] Jessica Katz, [Joseph W. Polisi and Crown Prince of Japan] Peter Schaaf, [American Brass Quintet, 1999] Peter Schaaf, [Michael Kahn and Candace M. Edwards] Jessica Katz, [The Mahabharata production] Jessica Katz, [Bass trombone student] Henry Grossman

ACKNOWLEDGMENTS

ABOVE ALL, we would like to thank Susan Lacy, executive producer and creator of *American Masters*. Susan is a mentor, visionary, and colleague who guided the Juilliard film from dream to reality and gave us never-ending support as well as the benefit of her insight and unparalleled experience. Her high standards and commitment to the art of filmmaking is unmatched, and we, as filmmakers, are proud to be part of her *American Masters* family.

We also gratefully acknowledge the people at Thirteen/WNET New York, whose ongoing support of great programming makes us optimistic about the future of public television in America. In particular, we would like to thank Bill Baker, Tamara Robinson, Jac Venza, Cindy Leff, and Joe Basile.

We thank the many brilliant members of the staff of *American Masters* and of this film's production team, who helped bring the Juilliard documentary to life. We salute each member of our production crew with respect and affection, especially Karen Bernstein, producer; Bob Richman, camera; J.T. Takagi, sound; Michael Weingrad, associate producer; and Karen Sim, editor. We also thank those with good advice and a colleague's keen eye—Sam Pollard, Charlotte Zwerin, Jamie Redford, Rachael Horovitz, Christopher Noey, Bruce Brubaker, and Tamar Hacker.

The opportunity to enter the world of The Juilliard School is a gift granted to very few. We explored this world not only with our camera, but also with our ears, our eyes, our hearts. At the end of our year, we wished we had studied at Juilliard, ourselves—wrapped in its support, reaching for its standards, and immersed in the collective knowledge and experience that it shares so freely and fully.

Our deepest gratitude goes to Joseph W. Polisi, the president of the Juilliard School, for his support and guidance. He opened Juilliard's doors to *American Masters* in a groundbreaking gesture that shows his respect for the past, his stewardship of the present, and his vision for the future of this great educational institution.

While we thank and acknowledge *everyone* at Juilliard—administrators, support staff, faculty, and students—we must give special acknowledgment to Mary Rodgers Guettel, Michael Kahn, Frank Corsaro, Yoheved Kaplinsky, Cynthia Hoffman, Katherine Hood, Otto-Werner Mueller, Bob Taibbi, Janet Kessin, and Jenna Soleo.

We offer deeply felt tributes and thanks to the late Dorothy DeLay and the late Benjamin Harkarvy, who helped us immeasurably throughout our filmmaking process—we join with everyone at Juilliard and so many others around the world in feeling their loss. We celebrate their life and the great gifts they gave to their students and the world of performing arts.

In the research for the film and book, we relied upon Jane Gottlieb and Jeni Dahmus, the wise and generous guardians of the Juilliard library and archives. We only touched the surface of the incredible range of resources and archival materials in Juilliard's impressive and fascinating collections.

In producing the film and book, a conscious decision was made to draw only from the experience of people directly involved with Juilliard, past and present. The lion's share of the text in this book is drawn from original interviews conducted for the film. The gifted people whose reflections are included in the book spoke from experience, from memory, and from their hearts. For every voice represented here, there are so many others—people whose association with Juilliard also informed our knowledge and understanding of the school, and whose talent, wisdom, and experience are shared *daily* throughout the world. We are so grateful to the artists we interviewed: Jane Adams, Emanuel Ax, Milton Babbitt, Morena Baccarin, Christine Baranski, Pina Bausch, Edward Bilous, Joseph Bloch, Omar Butler, Jeffrey Carlson, Julie Choi, Martha Clarke, Bill Conti, David Damrosch, Renée Fleming, Robert Garland, Thomas Gibson, Kelsey Grammer, Lisa Gay Hamilton, Marvin Hamlisch, Stephen McKinley Henderson, Bonnie Oda Homsey, Abdur-Rahim Jackson, Val Kilmer, Kevin Kline, Eriq La Salle, Rachel Lee, Pierre Lefevre,

James Levine, Laura Linney, Patti LuPone, Robert Mann, Bruce Marks, Wynton Marsalis, Audra McDonald, Tim Monich, Elizabeth Morgan, Gregory Mosher, Itzhak Perlman, Leontyne Price, Paula Robison, Mary Lou Rosato, Nadja Salerno-Sonnenberg, Marian Seldes, Leonard Slatkin, Mark Snow, Mary-Joan Negro Snow, Norman Snow, Kevin Spacey, Muriel Topaz, William Vacchiano, Diane Venora, Bradley Whitford, John Williams, Robert Neff Williams, Robin Williams, Sarah Wolfson, Moni Yakim, Anne Louise Zachry, Eugenia Zukerman, and Ellen Taaffe Zwilich. Thank you.

M.C., A.S.

As producer and director of the film and author of this book, I thank first and foremost my coauthor, Amy Schewel. I thank in particular my father, Ivan Chermayeff, whose beautiful titles grace the opening and close of the film and whose knowledge and vision have guided me in my life and supported me as we produced the book. I send thanks and undying love to my mother, Sara, who always makes me feel that everything I do is worthwhile and important. Love and admiration to my sisters, Catherine and Sasha, and my brother, Sam—and to Jane Chermayeff, who is always a voice of reason in the late hours of too much work! Love and gratitude to those who always weather the storm with me—especially Rachael Horovitz, Jamie and Kyle Redford, Meg Thayer, Avery Kaufman, Christine Le Goff, Elizabeth and Gianni Vallino, Mitchell Block, Howell Gibbens, Ziad Doueiri, and Catherine Nieland.

M.C.

As coproducer of the film and coauthor of this book, I want to thank the film's producer and director, Maro Chermayeff, for an unforgettable, galvanizing experience. I thank my mother, Marjorie Gordon, and my sister, Judith Gordon, and so many other supportive and insightful family, friends, and colleagues, especially Ilene Guttmacher, Maurice Berger and Marvin Heiferman, Patricia Falk, Mireille Mosler and Zwi Wasserstein, Mason Klein and Elizabeth Sacre, Jill Silverman van Coenegrachts, Tim Wallach and Fleur Fairman, Clay and Katharine Andres, Kenneth Greif, Lee M. Hendler, Susan P. Fillion, Kathryn Hillman, Amy and Marc Meadows, Colleen O'Connor, Mark Atkinson, Maryann Marrapodi, Dr. Joseph Finkelstein, Elliot and Rosel Schewel, Leo and Jean Gordon, and Henry Schewel.

A.S.

The Juilliard School

Program for concert celebrating Juilliard's move to Lincoln Center, Alice Tully Hall, October 5, 1969

David Ogden Stiers and Patti LuPone, Drama Division Group 1, in *The School for Scandal*, 1971

Joseph W. Polisi with the Crown Prince of Japan, c. 1987

Van Cliburn, a Juilliard piano student studying under Rosina Lhévinne, wins first place in the first Tchaikovsky competition in Moscow, making the name Juilliard known world-wide. He is welcomed back to New York with a ticker-tape parade.

Composer Peter Mennin assumes Juilliard presidency, November 1, serving until his death in 1983. Mennin oversees the school's move to Lincoln Center, establishes the Drama Division, the Juilliard American Opera Center (now the Juilliard Opera Center), and the Doctor of Musical Arts program.

Doctor of Musical Arts degree program is established.

The school's name is changed to The Juilliard School to reflect its broadened mission in educating musicians, dancers, and actors.

Juilliard moves to its present home at Lincoln Center in a building designed by Pietro Belluschi, Eduardo Catalano, and Helge Westermann.

The first class of Drama Division students (Group 1) graduates and forms The Acting Company with John Houseman.

Joseph W. Polisi, author, scholar, administrator, and performing bassoonist, is appointed Juilliard's sixth president. Polisi goes on to oversee the establishment of new student services and alumni programs, educational outreach programs, a revised curriculum with new emphasis on humanities and liberal arts education, and the development of interdisciplinary programs to foster greater interaction among the school's divisions.

1958   **1961**   **1962**   **1963**   **1966**   **1968**   **1969**   **1970**   **1972**   **1976**   **1984**

William Schuman is named president of Lincoln Center for the Performing Arts, Inc., September 12. His appointment is effective January 1, 1962.

Bachelor of Music (BM) and Bachelor of Fine Arts degrees are instituted.

The Drama Division is established under the direction of John Houseman (1968–76), with Michel Saint-Denis as consultant.

Juilliard's new American Opera Center presents its first production in the Juilliard Theater, Igor Stravinsky's *A Rake's Progress,* conducted by Erich Leinsdorf, April 23.

Alan Schneider is appointed director of the Drama Division (1976–79). He is succeeded by Michael Langham (1979–92).

John Houseman at his desk at Juilliard

Bradley Whitford, Drama Division Group 14, c. 1985